THE FORBIDDEN ROAD

Dave Gustaveson

D0029195

YWAM Publishing
A Ministry of Youth With A Mission
P.O. Box 55787, Seattle, WA 98155
(206) 771-1153

████████████████ the publishing ministry of Youth With A Mission. Youth With A Mission (YWAM) is an international missionary organization of Christians from many denominations dedicated to presenting Jesus Christ to this generation. To this end, YWAM has focused its efforts in three main areas: 1) Training and equipping believers for their part in fulfilling the Great Commission (Matthew 28:19). 2) Personal evangelism. 3) Mercy ministry (medical and relief work).

For a free catalog of books and materials write or call:
YWAM Publishing
P.O. Box 55787, Seattle, WA 98155
(206) 771-1153 or (800) 922-2143
email adress: 75701.2772 @ compuserve.com

The Forbidden Road

Copyright © 1996 by David Gustaveson

Published by Youth With A Mission Publishing
P.O. Box 55787
Seattle, WA 98155

ISBN 0-927545-89-6

Printed in the United States of America.

To
my loving
MOM
who sacrificed
countless hours praying
for my conversion
which happened
on a
Mother's
Day

Other

REEL KIDS
Adventures

Available at your local Christian bookstore or
YWAM Publishing
1(800) 922-2143

Acknowledgments

Prayer is the key to moving the heart and hand of God in any situation. The countless hours my wonderful mom spent in prayer for me were instrumental in bringing me to Jesus. Who knows where I would be today were it not for her unwavering commitment to stand in prayer for me.

As we look around this hurting world, we see nations that need that kind of intercession. With the right kind of prayer cover, we would see nations fall at Jesus' feet. Korea is fast becoming a Christian nation because of millions of praying Koreans around the world.

The Communist world has been shaken to the core because of prayer. This book is about the miracle of China. Many have stood in the gap for this huge nation, and God is on the move. I believe China can come into its finest hour as each saint continues to hold it up to God.

A very special thanks to John Davidson, one of my closest friends and fellow prayer warriors. His many bike trips into China added much to the plot of this book.

Also, special thanks to Suzanne Howe, who takes great interest in my books, spending lots of time reading the manuscripts and adding insight. Thanks to Alexis Wilson, whose journey from Beijing to the Great Wall contributed spice to the story.

Thanks to Paul Kauffman for his book on China. It is filled with many insights. Also, thanks to my in-laws, whose five trips into China have brought them a wealth of experience.

And of course, I need to mention the diligent and excellent work of those at YWAM Publishing. Also to my editor Marit Holmgren and to Frank Ordaz for his great cover illustrations.

May God help His Church to rise in prayer in this final hour like never before.

Table of Contents

Chapter 1

The Accident

"Look out!"

Jeff Caldwell gasped in surprise, hearing his younger sister's scream shatter the momentary silence. Straining his blue eyes in wide astonishment, he stared straight ahead.

"Stop!" he cried. "Stop!"

Brakes screeched and whined as the taxi skidded to a halt. They had barely missed two crumpled kids buried under a pair of overturned bikes.

Concern filled Mindy's face. "They must be hurt pretty bad."

Jeff nodded, fighting back panic. The fifteen-year-old fixed his eyes on the distressed riders sprawled

9

in the middle of the Hong Kong road. Their arms and legs were bloodied. His heart jumped as a red double-decker bus roared by, barely missing them.

"We have to get them off the road," Jeff cried. "They're going to get hit."

Mindy reached for the door, her brown eyes growing bigger by the second. By now, they all but filled her brown-rimmed glasses.

Desperately, Jeff forced himself into action. "I'll get the first aid kit."

He reached frantically into his duffle bag. The last thing he wanted to see today was a bike accident. For months, the Reel Kids Club had trained for a seven-day bike trek into mysterious China. Their goal was to make a video to inspire kids around the world to go on mission adventures. They were to start the ride tomorrow. Even now, he and Mindy were on their way to meet the others at a bike rental shop in the New Territory of Hong Kong. Witnessing a bike crash was not the way to start the trip.

"Let's go," Mindy urged impatiently, her blond ponytail swinging to and fro as she leaped from the blue Mercedes taxi. She grabbed the first aid kit from Jeff and raced toward the hurting kids.

Jeff was right behind her. He would let Mindy lead on this one. His thirteen-year-old sister was gifted in helping hurting people. As he ran to the middle of the road, Jeff noticed the taxi driver pull off to the side and park. He wondered if the driver would keep the meter running, charging them for the delay.

His heart leapt when he looked into the frightened faces of the young bikers. The club's mission on this trip was not just to make a video, but to show God's love to all the people they met. He had prayed for the Chinese people for so many months. He almost felt the riders' painful cuts and bruises when he saw the small-framed Chinese girl crying.

Quickly, Jeff moved the bikes out of the way. Mindy knelt down beside the riders.

"Are you okay?" she asked gently.

"I think so," the young girl replied, wiping her eyes. "We scraped ourselves pretty bad."

"We better get off the road," Jeff urged. "Do you think you can stand up?"

The bleeding riders nodded, still dazed from their crash. Carefully, Jeff and Mindy helped them hobble to the side of the road.

"It looks like surface cuts," Mindy assessed after a moment. "We'll need something to clean them with."

At that instant, a Chinese woman hurried over carrying a wet cloth. She handed it to Mindy. By now, a small and curious crowd had gathered.

Gently, Mindy dabbed their arms, adding disinfectant from the first aid kit. Jeff smiled, knowing she had things under control. Though Mindy was the researcher for their media club, she was a natural when it came to ministering to people's physical needs. Her first love was journalism, but she had always had an interest in the medical field.

Jeff looked at his watch. 10:30 a.m. He knew the rest of the team would worry if they didn't show up soon. But they couldn't leave the riders there without helping. Just then, he spotted the frustrated taxi driver pull away, not bothering to collect his fare. Now they had lost their ride.

Watching Mindy carefully clean the scrapes, Jeff

thought about the days to come. Going on a bike adventure into Communist China was not without risk. They could even face arrest if caught with Bibles. The government was controlled by Communism, and its borders weren't called the Bamboo Curtain for nothing. Jeff had prayed for months that the team would be allowed to enter the ancient land.

They had arrived in Hong Kong on a hot July Sunday, and today, Monday, had been set aside for bike training with their Chinese translator. Tuesday was the day they were waiting for—the day the club would fly into Beijing.

Jeff and Mindy had joined the Reel Kids Club soon after moving to Los Angeles. Their leader, Warren Russell, headed the communications department at their high school. When he formed the club, he envisioned taking kids around the world to share the Gospel and at the same time produce videos of their adventures to practice their communication skills and inspire other kids. And that's just what the Reel Kids did. Even when the club returned home from trips, there was always lots to do to edit the film and prepare to show it to churches and youth groups.

One thing Warren had stressed in the club was that God had given everyone special skills they could contribute to the team. Jeff's best friend, K.J., was the club's cameraman. For his age, he was excellent. He was responsible for the video equipment they borrowed from the school.

Mindy was their ace reporter. Her love for information made her an excellent researcher for their international adventures. Her inquisitive mind asked all the right questions. Jeff was almost convinced she slept with her laptop computer.

Jeff's own dream was to set up a high tech video production company after he graduated from college. He loved being on the front end of the camera. He guessed communications ran in his family. Jeff and Mindy's dad was a successful TV anchorman for a large Los Angeles station, and their mom worked as a news correspondent.

Through the club, Jeff, Mindy and K.J. had been to parts of the world a lot of kids never even hear about. Whether they went to Istanbul, Manila, Mombassa, or deep into the Amazon jungle, their adventures were always filled with heart-pounding excitement.

This time, the club had been invited by Mike Gates, director of World Bike Tours, to journey with him into China to produce a video to recruit kids for future bike trips. Jeff and the others had trained on mountain bikes for weeks in Los Angeles, preparing for the challenging ride through mountains and villages from Beijing to the Great Wall of China and back. A trip on roads watched carefully by the secret police.

Jeff shook off the thought of secret police. "I'm not being very helpful, am I, sis? How you doing?"

Mindy answered without taking her attention away from her patients. "Thank goodness they're not hurt badly. It's just minor cuts and scrapes. I'll be finished in a minute."

"How did you crash anyway?" Jeff asked the Chinese boy.

The boy smiled sheepishly. "It was my fault. After

renting the bikes, we headed a little fast down this hill. I hit the brakes hard, and the front tire locked up. After my bike flipped, my sister crashed right into me."

The boy's eyes sparkled. "Hong Kong people are not very good riders. The streets are too busy to ride bikes, except out here."

Jeff smiled warmly. Together, they watched Mindy cover the girl's worst scrapes with some large band-aids. Thinking about the miles of biking ahead, Jeff uttered a quick prayer for protection.

"There," Mindy smiled confidently. "I think you'll be okay now."

"Please be careful," Jeff warned, as the brother and sister stood and righted their bikes. "The cars are racing by pretty fast around here."

"We will be," the Chinese girl promised.

Suddenly, Jeff remembered that their taxi had left already. "How far is the bike rental place from here?"

The bandaged girl smiled, pulling her long black hair out of her face. Her dark eyes shone in the sunlight. "It's about three blocks up the road."

"That's all?" Mindy laughed in relief. "We can walk that."

Everyone grinned, suddenly shy.

"Thanks for helping us," the Chinese boy said at last, climbing slowly aboard his bike. "We hope you have a nice visit."

Watching the brother and sister wobble away on their bikes, Jeff tried not to chuckle. "I hope they'll be okay."

"Me too," Mindy said. "It was great to speak English with them."

"Yeah. That won't be the case once we get inside

China. We'll need our translator."

Mindy nodded. "We better get going. Warren and the others will think we got lost." She paused, looking worried. "I hope we don't have any accidents. Mike says our interpreter doesn't know how to ride very well."

"That's why we're taking him out for some practice."

Minutes later, Jeff and Mindy arrived at the wooden shack that housed the rental shop. Colored mountain bikes lined the bike rack in front, ready for riding. Jeff's heart fluttered with excitement. Their adventure was getting closer.

Glancing around, he saw his best friend, K.J., busy filming the area. K.J.'s hands held the Canon Hi-8 camcorder securely, the camera bag bobbing against his body.

Jeff smiled, watching his buddy. His slick, black hair, constant smile, and dark, mischievous eyes gave him the appearance that he was always up to something. Kyle James Baxter had been Jeff's best friend ever since the Caldwells moved to Baldwin Heights. Never afraid to venture into something new, K.J. loved being on the cutting edge. If his adventurous spirit got him in trouble sometimes, it was more often an asset to the club. That spirit was one of the things that made him a great cameraman. For a fourteen-year-old, he had a steady hand and a good eye. He didn't miss much.

When he saw Jeff, K.J. lowered the camcorder.

"Boy, you guys are late. What did you do—take a tour of Hong Kong along the way?"

Jeff eyed Mindy. He knew K.J. had a way of making her blood boil. Seeing her face start to redden, Jeff quickly gathered Warren and Mike and explained what had happened.

Mike looked like he belonged at the bike shop. With wavy brown hair, bushy eyebrows and dark brown eyes, he had to be six feet tall. His husky, athletic build revealed hundreds of miles of biking. Mike had started World Bike Tours with a similar vision to the Reel Kids Club. It was a powerful way to get kids to forget about themselves and discover the adventure of giving their lives away for the Gospel. He planned to send lots of teams around the world during summers and school breaks.

Warren was in his early thirties, but some people thought he looked young enough to be a club member. He wasn't married, and his commitment to the mission of the Reel Kids Club was whole-hearted. More and more Jeff came to see that Warren's deep love for God and compassion for people were what guided him. He had taught Jeff a lot more than communications. He was a true servant-leader, willing to let others step out to lead. A "coach" who got joy from watching his team play. A man quick to acknowledge when he had made a mistake.

"We've got some cool bikes picked out for you guys to ride today," Mike said, pointing to a group of bikes in front of the shop.

"K.J. gets the pink one, of course," Mindy teased.

K.J. grinned. "Actually, that's for you."

"Jeff," Warren said, "I need to get the visas this

afternoon, so I'm putting you and Mike in charge today. Please be careful."

Jeff smiled. "We will. And we'll pray that everything goes fine with the visas."

Soon after Warren left, their Chinese interpreter, Harold, pedaled up on a red mountain bike. Wearing purple bike shorts and a matching spandex shirt, he was dressed to ride, but he was clearly very nervous.

Jeff was just thankful Mike had been able to find an interpreter. He smiled, hoping a friendly face would help the college student relax. "We're glad you're going with us. We couldn't do this trip without you."

Harold smiled back, his big, dark eyes expressive. "I just hope I can handle the mountains. We don't bike very much. In Hong Kong, we go everywhere by car or bus."

"You'll be fine," K.J. offered. "We'll have you in shape in a couple hours."

"Watch out, Harold," Mindy said, rolling her eyes.

Jeff grinned. "Just think, tomorrow we'll be taking Bibles into Red China. Only the power of God's Word can bring down the Bamboo Curtain Communism has built."

Thinking of this filled K.J. with excitement. "I've waited a long time for this. I've seen smugglers do this in movies. Now I get to do it for God."

Mindy took a deep breath. "What if we get caught?" she asked.

"Good question," Mike said. "Christians take Bibles in every day. If someone is caught, they normally just give a strong warning and take away the

Bibles. Unless we get the wrong border guard."

"Well, if K.J.'s with us, he'll find a way to get us arrested."

K.J. smirked. "I hear the border guards are on special lookout for blondes with ponytails."

Mindy just laughed. If she teased K.J., she guessed she had to let him tease her.

Jeff looked at Mike. "Now that everybody's here, why don't we get going?"

Biking down the highway, Jeff had to adjust to the traffic going the opposite direction. He was glad it wasn't that way in China. Training up ahead with Harold, Mike had set a medium pace for their practice run. Jeff, K.J. and Mindy followed close behind, putting into practice what they had learned on their training trips at home.

Looking ahead, Jeff was glad to see that the ride would be fairly easy pedaling. There was some traffic to deal with, but only a few small hills to climb. Staring in delight toward mainland China, he realized how close he was to the massive Communist nation. He felt excitement building, remembering what Mindy had taught them about this ancient land. It was the oldest living civilization!

Jeff realized how blessed he was to be on a special mission for God. Meeting Warren had radically changed his life. Now he wanted to spend the rest of his life going on adventures for God.

Suddenly, Jeff's thoughts were jarred as a big double-decker bus rushed by, creating a forceful wind.

Mindy yelled out. "Be careful, you guys. Those kids we helped earlier were pretty skinned up."

"Don't worry," K.J. said. "We've got it under control."

Passing a parked bus, the team coasted down a slight hill. Jeff squirmed on his seat, trying to get comfortable. He had a funny feeling something was wrong.

Just then, another large, red double-decker bus raced by, filled with passengers. As it slowed, Jeff figured it was preparing to pull over to a roadside bus stop. Looking ahead, he saw Mike speed up to beat the bus on the inside. Harold was pedaling fast, slightly ahead.

Jeff breathed a sigh of relief as Mike slowed down, realizing he couldn't make it. He thought Harold would do the same, but he didn't. Almost blindly, he headed for danger. Suddenly, the bus swerved sharply toward the curb. Harold sped up, trying to get past. Jeff felt a cold chill creep from the nape of his neck down to the base of his spine.

He knew Harold wasn't going to make it.

Chapter 2

Roadblocks

Jeff's mind raced. He felt totally helpless. Though Mike screamed loudly, the roar from the bus deafened Harold to his cries. Harold sped ahead. When Mindy saw what was happening, she screamed in horror. Everyone knew he didn't have a chance.

Jeff held his breath as the bus inched closer to the curb. Maybe, just maybe, Harold could squeeze through.

"He's not going to make it," K.J. cried. "He's going to get hit."

Jeff's thoughts flashed back to the young Hong Kong riders. If only the bus driver would see Harold.

In those split seconds, Jeff prayed intensely. He knew a crash like this could be fatal. He heard himself scream as the bus almost clipped Harold. The panicked rider looked back, terror on his face. Finally the driver saw him. Slamming on the brakes, he tried to head off disaster. Tires squealed and screamed, as if they too recognized the sudden danger. But the bus was too heavy to stop.

Jeff heard a light but horrible thud. Harold's bike had been bumped and was totally out of control. Helpless, he headed straight for the curb. Jeff closed his eyes, not wanting to see. He knew Harold needed a miracle. This would be a lot worse than the earlier accident.

Thump! Harold's front tire hit the curb at full speed, and he flung end over end off the bike. His helmet and upper body smashed sickeningly into a nearby light pole.

Too late, the bus swerved to a full stop. Mike jumped off his bike and ran to Harold, who lay deathly still. Filled with dread, Jeff and the others followed.

"K.J.," Mike ordered, "find someone to help you call an ambulance. We have to get him to a hospital."

Mike tried to talk to Harold, but he was unconscious. Standing there in shock, Jeff prayed. Everyone stared at each other in disbelief.

At last, Harold groaned, slowly opening his eyes. By now, a small crowd had gathered. People watched from the bus as the driver rushed to join them at Harold's side.

Jeff looked into Harold's eyes. Though dazed, Harold tried to focus his vision. Looking over his slumped body, Jeff saw only a little blood, mostly from cuts on his arms. He couldn't believe it. It had to be a miracle.

Mike continued talking to Harold. "Where do you hurt?" he asked.

"My arms," Harold moaned. "I can't move them."

Jeff's heart jumped. Surely Harold wouldn't be paralyzed!

The whining siren of the approaching ambulance brought icy chills to his spine. He wondered again how this could be happening. His emotions fluttered wildly. Ironically, he suddenly remembered the plane's landing over Hong Kong Harbor. His mind filled with memories of colored lights, tall buildings, and large ships on the water below. Though he had been exhausted from the long trip, it was a happy and breathtaking moment.

Now his mind was confused. As the ambulance pulled up, Jeff stared at the mangled bike resting beside them on the sidewalk. It hurt him to hear Harold groan in pain. Mindy and Mike attempted to reassure Harold, but Jeff knew he must be terribly frightened. Jeff tried to focus his thoughts. He knew he had to trust that God would bring good out of this tragedy.

While the ambulance attendants assessed Harold's injuries, Mike organized the team. "They'll take him to the hospital a few miles from here. Jeff and Mindy, you take a taxi and follow. K.J., you'll need to stay with the bikes, while I ride back to the rental shop and get a truck to come back for the other bikes. We'll meet Jeff and Mindy at the hospital later."

Jeff tried to gather himself. "What about Warren? We need to call him."

Mike nodded. "When you get to the hospital, call the YMCA. Leave a message for Warren. I'll call Harold's parents when I get to the bike shop."

They turned to watch the attendants shift Harold onto the stretcher. Jeff knew they had to be careful. If his neck was broken, the wrong move could cause permanent paralysis.

Still in a state of shock, Jeff wrote down the name of the hospital given him by the ambulance driver, while Mindy hailed a cab. As the taxi followed the ambulance into traffic, Jeff looked back. There K.J. sat, alone with the riderless mountain bikes.

Rushing into the hospital, Jeff noticed a large open ward filled with doctors, nurses and patients. Heading to the waiting room was not a new experience for the club. Jeff remembered the other times and places God had performed a miracle. They needed one now.

In the waiting room, Jeff and Mindy sat silently, both staring at the floor.

After a while, Mindy looked up. "If we don't get a translator, does that mean we can't go?"

"That's up to Mike. It's his call since he invited us." Jeff retreated into silence, wishing Warren were there. He would know what to do next.

"Let's pray together for Harold," Mindy suggested. "It'll make us feel better, too."

Jeff smiled to himself. His sister was pretty wise sometimes.

It was late afternoon when K.J. and Mike got there.

"Any news on Harold?" Mike asked right away.

Jeff shook his head. "We were told to wait here for the doctor's report."

"We finally got the bikes back," K.J. said, explaining why they were so late. "It took a while for the truck to come."

Mike sat down. "Harold's parents got the news and will be here soon. What about Warren?"

"We left a message," Mindy said. "He must be busy with the visas or..."

Before she finished, Warren hurried in. Jeff jumped up to greet him. After a few minutes, Warren was caught up on the details of the accident.

"What about the visas?" Jeff asked, wanting to keep the mission alive.

Warren frowned.

"What's wrong?" K.J. wondered for all of them. The whole club leaned forward in their chairs, waiting to hear.

"I arrived, and the office was closed. Everything closed at noon today."

"Does that mean we can't go?" K.J. asked.

"No. It just means I have to return first thing in the morning. We catch our plane tomorrow at one. That doesn't leave much time."

Jeff felt discouragement well up within him. He knew the battle was getting hot.

Just then, a doctor approached them, looking very somber.

"Is he going to be okay?" Mindy begged.

"Well, he won't suffer any paralysis. And he's regained feeling in his arms."

Mindy smiled. "Does that mean he'll be okay?"

The doctor frowned. "He hit that pole really hard. He has a head concussion and a dislocated shoulder. He won't be riding a bike for a few months."

Mindy's face fell.

"Can we see him?" Warren asked.

"Only for a few minutes. We're waiting for his parents to come. Then we need to reset his shoulder."

Quickly, the team filed in to see Harold. He began apologizing for the accident, but Jeff encouraged him, and everyone prayed together. Moments passed quickly, and when Harold's parents came, the team left them alone with their son.

Back in the waiting room, Jeff was full of questions. Turning to Mike, he raised his eyebrows. "Poor Harold. I feel really bad for him."

Mike nodded. "I hope he doesn't blame himself too much for the accident."

"Can we go without him?" K.J. asked.

Mike answered honestly. "Without a translator, we can't do much at all. And we wouldn't get good footage."

Jeff felt the energy drain from his tired body. He had dreamed for months about this trip. "Everything seems to be going wrong," he said flatly. "First Harold, then the visas. What's next?"

"Nothing I hope," Mike said. "My host in Beijing might be able to find us another translator. But when I asked before, he said he didn't have one. We can try again. People inside China are much more skilled at biking."

"How do we contact him?"

"We'll fax him tonight and see what he can do."

"Where are you going to get a fax machine?"

Mike chuckled. "That's not hard in Hong Kong. The Chinese are on the cutting edge of electronic communication. They probably have one at the YMCA. For sure at the nearby Peninsula Hotel."

Standing inside the Peninsula Hotel, Jeff was overwhelmed by its elegance. With its beautiful lighting, colorful wall coverings and plush furniture, the lobby was breathtaking.

Inside, nicely dressed guests strolled by. Outside, Jeff could see tourists being carried along in rickshaws, two-wheeled buggies, each pulled by a Chinese man. From the looks of the hotel lobby, Jeff figured it would cost a small fortune for a room.

Gazing out the large windows at the glittering lights across the harbor of Hong Kong, he understood why so many people liked to journey to Hong Kong. It was beautiful. It was also a free land, an island given to Britain by China in 1842. An island that was booming economically, in contrast to its Communist motherland. An island filled with Westerners living and vacationing in the exotic and exciting atmosphere of the East.

"Let's hope Thomas is near his fax machine," Mike said, jarring Jeff out of his thoughts.

"Yeah," Jeff agreed. "Let's hope so."

"Let's also hope no one else is near it. I tried to be careful with my wording."

Jeff nodded, waiting impatiently. Moments later, the fax machine slowly pushed out a message. Finally, the page dropped into the tray.

Mike read quickly, his smile fading. "It doesn't look good. Thomas says he doesn't think it's possible to find anyone on such short notice. But he'll work on it and fax us in the morning."

Jeff groaned. "We need to have a prayer meeting."

The sun invaded the Tuesday morning sky, scattering the darkness and filling Jeff with a new hope. He was glad the club had agreed to meet together for early morning prayer.

After breakfast, they gathered in Warren, K.J. and Jeff's room. Mike had just arrived.

Jeff looked at the others. "We're not going to be defeated. God has everything in control. We just need to pray."

Everyone bowed their heads. Jeff led out.

"Father in heaven, in the past few months, You have shown me Your heart for China. We ask You to show Your greatness in providing our visas and a translator. Open doors as we prepare to reach out to this giant nation."

After a good season of prayer, everyone said amen in unison. Then Warren left to get the visas. Jeff and Mike stayed back to finish packing, while K.J. and Mindy headed to Kowloon, the famous shopping district, to get extra parts for the bikes.

"How long will it take to get to the airport?" Jeff asked.

Mike sat back on his chair, deep in thought. "About thirty minutes if the traffic isn't bad."

"What time are we supposed to be there?"

"They want us there two hours early. But I don't see how we're going to do that. That means we would have to leave for the airport at ten o'clock."

"Can Warren get the visas that fast?"

"I don't think so. But we prayed, didn't we?"

Jeff looked at his watch. It was 8:30. "We better check that fax."

Mike nodded nervously. "I hope it's good news."

They walked silently to the Peninsula Hotel. When the receptionist saw them, she smiled warmly, handing them the new fax.

Slowly, Mike read the words aloud. "Sorry. No one is available."

Chapter 3

The Bamboo Curtain

Jeff felt anger rise up in his spirit. He couldn't understand why everything was going wrong. Their prayers hadn't been answered.

"What shall we do now?" he mumbled, trying to get control of his attitude.

"We have to make a decision," Mike said. "Maybe we're not supposed to go today. That could be why Warren didn't get the visas."

Jeff felt outraged at the thought. "I'm sure this is an attack of darkness. I've prayed over and over for China. Let's go back and do it one more time."

When Jeff and Mike got back to the YMCA, K.J.

and Mindy had just returned. Jeff explained their situation.

"Maybe we're not supposed to go," Mindy said. "We could always visit Beijing and travel by car."

"Can't we hire a translator?" K.J. asked.

"Yeah. But it won't be the same as finding someone who believes in our mission," Jeff said, feeling defeated.

Mindy tried to smile. "Let's pray, you guys." Everyone bowed their heads as she led out. "Father, we stand against the powers of darkness who want to keep China hidden from Your truth. Lord, we look to You."

"Lord," Mike prayed, "we understand that Harold can't come with us, but we pray for his healing and ask You to bless his willingness to help our team."

When the team had finished, Jeff looked at the others. "Let's give this to God."

The minutes flew by. It was already ten, and there was still no sign of Warren.

"I can't stand this kind of pressure," Mindy complained. "Why don't we just wait until we get a translator."

Jeff fought back frustration. "Look, you guys. If we delay much longer, we won't be able to go anywhere except Beijing. We leave for home next Monday. That's only a few days away."

Mike nodded in agreement. "And it might be hard to catch another flight to Beijing."

"Well," K.J. muttered, "I wouldn't mind going to Kowloon again. It's the best shopping district in Hong Kong—the electronic stuff is amazing. I'd sure like to get some Chinese firecrackers, too."

Mindy rolled her eyes. "Why do you want firecrackers? I read that some people here believe that the loud noise frightens away the evil spirits."

"Maybe that would help right now."

"Very funny. You're the only loud noise around here."

Jeff gave K.J. and Mindy an exasperated look. "You guys, if we can't get along, we'll never make it to China."

Jeff looked at his watch again. 10:30. "What's taking Warren so long?" he wondered aloud.

"Maybe he stopped in Kowloon," Mindy laughed.

Jeff and K.J. were not amused.

Jeff paced back and forth, aware of each passing minute. It was 10:43 when the phone rang, startling everyone.

Quickly, Jeff grabbed it. A big smile unfurled across his face. "It's the hotel receptionist. She has another fax from Thomas."

"Let's get it," Mike cried. "Maybe he found somebody." K.J. and Mindy stayed behind in case Warren returned. Mike and Jeff raced outside, heading for the hotel lobby. Hurrying to the desk, they looked like kids in a candy store. The receptionist handed Mike the fax.

Mike read the words aloud. "Amazing answer to your situation."

Jeff's pulse quickened.

"I found two translators. College students available for next week. Looking forward to your arrival."

Jeff couldn't believe the words. Filled with a new energy he looked at his watch. Eleven o'clock.

"Let's get out of here," Mike said. "Maybe Warren's back. We can still barely make it."

Jeff was beside himself with joy. God had come through. He couldn't wait to share the news. When he ran into their room at the YMCA, he felt like singing a thousand songs of praise. There was Warren, standing in the room with K.J. and Mindy.

"Boy," Jeff said, "are we glad to see you!"

"It took a minor miracle, but I got the visas."

"And Thomas found two good translators," Jeff shouted triumphantly. "Let's get out of here. Maybe we can still catch our plane."

Everyone grabbed their luggage and ran outside to the road.

"Let's try to fit everything into one taxi," Warren directed.

"I don't know," Mindy said doubtfully. "Have you seen K.J.'s packages?"

"Some of this is for the bikes, okay?"

"What else is there?" Mindy teased.

"Some gifts for my family. I'll leave them with Thomas when we get to Beijing."

"I hope you got the right parts for the bikes," Jeff said. "I don't want to get stuck in the middle of China with a flat tire."

As if it knew they were in a hurry, a taxi pulled to the side of the road, screeching its tires as it stopped. Quickly, the club piled in.

When they got to the main highway, Jeff didn't

like what he saw. The traffic was at a total standstill.

"This looks like a freeway in Los Angeles," K.J. laughed. No one responded.

Jeff felt frustration growing once again. Trying to calm himself, he stirred up his faith. "I know we'll make it," he said boldly. "We've got to."

The taxi moved at a crawl. Jeff checked the time again. It was already 11:45. "How much longer is it?" he asked.

Mike turned in his seat, beads of sweat dotting his forehead. "If we travel normal speed, it could take thirty to forty minutes."

Jeff felt slapped by the words.

Swiftly, K.J. pulled out his camera "Maybe it's time for an interview."

Jeff wanted to protest, but suddenly he grinned. "That's a good idea. We need something to take our minds off the time. Besides, it'll make good footage of the beginning of our trip."

Mindy liked the idea, too. "We could start by talking about Marco Polo. He's the one who discovered an isolated, out-of-touch China hundreds of years ago. When he came back, he went on about the beautiful land, its people, and the potential for trade. Word got out, and other nations sent delegations there. From what I read, a lot of China's troubles started after that because there were so many changes so fast."

"That's amazing," K.J. said. "I thought Marco Polo was only the name of that game we play in the swimming pool."

Everyone tried to laugh at K.J.'s humor. Seconds later, he had the camera rolling. Jeff asked Mike some questions about World Bike Tours. After a while, K.J. turned the camera to Mindy, who talked about Marco Polo and modern China.

Finished, K.J. reluctantly stared at his watch. It was 12:15.

"How much longer?" Mindy asked.

"Soon," Mike said. "I've never seen traffic like this on a Tuesday afternoon."

Jeff groaned. It didn't look good.

Jeff spotted the airport at 12:25. He felt tension rising up inside, like an explosion ready to go off.

The taxi jerked to a stop in front of the airport terminal. The club members piled out, everyone grabbing their own stuff and running for the airport lounge.

Rushing toward the China Airline counter, Jeff stopped cold. A long line of people stood in their way.

"We'll never make it in that line," Mindy groaned.

"Let's get in line anyway," Jeff said stubbornly. "God will help us."

Just then an airline agent approached Warren. "What flight are you on?"

"The one o'clock flight to Beijing."

The man looked surprised. "I don't see how you can make it, but leave your bags here and come this way."

After checking their passports, the agent quickly

issued boarding passes. "You're lucky the plane isn't full. But you still may not make it. You'll really have to hurry."

Arriving at the jetway, Jeff looked around frantically. No one was at the ticket desk. He was just about to ask where everybody was when another agent strode up.

"Can I help you?" the man asked.

"We're supposed to be on this flight," Jeff said, struggling to keep his voice calm.

The agent shook his head. "I'm sorry. The door is shut, and the plane is backing out. You'll have to wait until tomorrow."

Jeff breathed hard from the long run. Looking at the others, he knew it was over. They, too, had surrendered to the words of defeat. Silently, the team headed for a place to sit.

They had just sat down on a row of plastic chairs when another agent walked off the jetway and into the lounge. She looked at their flushed faces and the carry-on bags piled at their feet.

"Were you trying to get on this flight?" she asked brightly.

"We're too late," Jeff moaned. "It's leaving."

"This is your lucky day," she beamed, happy to bring good news. "The captain forgot a package. The door is open again. You can just make it if you hurry."

Jeff thought he was dreaming. He knew it wasn't luck that got them on the plane.

With a great sigh of relief, everyone danced along the jetway to the plane. Ignoring the dirty looks from other passengers who thought they'd caused the delay, they put their bags away.

Totally exhausted, Jeff flopped into his seat. They'd given up hope just a little too early. After all it had taken to get them on this flight, he couldn't help but wonder what exciting things lay ahead.

It was seven o'clock when the pilot announced the plane's gradual descent into Beijing International Airport. Jeff had already put up his beverage tray and gathered his things into his duffle bag. He had dreamed of going to China for months. Now it was minutes away.

Grinning from ear to ear, Jeff leaned over to Mindy. "Now the exciting part of the trip begins."

"I just hope they don't search our backpacks," Mindy whispered. "If they find those Bibles, we could be in big trouble."

"God has taken us this far," Jeff said quietly. "He's more concerned about getting those Bibles to China than we are. I've even read stories of God blinding airport police when they've searched the luggage."

"We'll need Him to blind the guards," Mindy said. "Especially with K.J. with us."

K.J. smiled as he overheard. "Hey, Mindy, I heard the guards like to cut off ponytails and collect them."

"You guys," Jeff whispered, "cool it. We're getting close."

Walking off the plane, Jeff realized he was entering the most populated nation in the world. His heart was moved, thinking of this vast and ancient land. A land in transition, and yet a land with incredible history, amazing art, and an overabundance of travel destinations. A land with vast natural resources, limitless manpower and tremendous potential.

Jeff's heartbeat quickened as he observed all around him the beautiful Chinese people he had prayed for. Ironically, he sensed a strange heaviness he had never felt before. A deep darkness from an oppressive government, from Communism with all its controls and its strangling effects on the people. Yet Jeff knew this evil system was losing its grip on this land with great potential for God. Moving toward the immigration line, Mike cautioned everyone about how to respond to questions. As he waited his turn, Jeff looked around. Everything looked different. Empty and drab.

Finally, Jeff moved to the window. A Chinese official stared right at him, then at his passport. Jeff tried not to fidget. At last, the thud of the stamp hit his passport, and he was free to go. As the others made it through, he let out a sigh of relief.

"Now we have one more hurdle," Mike said.

"What's that?" Mindy asked.

"Getting through baggage inspection."

Nearing the front of the line, Jeff tried to stay calm. He hoped they wouldn't search the bottom of his backpack. It was filled with little Bibles.

When it was Jeff's turn, the officer abruptly stopped what he was doing. Jeff's heart sank. Angrily, the officer nodded to another man, who appeared to be his boss. The man rushed over.

Jeff smiled at him not knowing what else to do. The man wore a green, carefully pressed uniform, with one Red Chinese star on the shoulder and hat. He was short and stocky, with dark features and a scar that cut from his ear to his cheekbone.

"Are you from America?" he asked gruffly.

They all nodded.

"Let me see your passports," he demanded.

Jeff waited, fighting to control the panic he felt.

The man examined the documents, staring at each member in turn. "Please come with me."

Chapter 4

Warned

Jeff felt more and more uneasy. This man seemed to know everything about them. As they followed the man into a windowless room, Jeff's mind flashed to the other times he had been stopped at foreign airports. Obeying Jesus to take the Gospel to all the world was rarely easy.

Jeff looked questioningly at Warren. Warren shrugged. He didn't have any idea what was happening either. K.J. held his camera tightly. Jeff was glad he had sense enough not to run it.

The man led them to a row of old wooden benches along the far wall. Jeff looked around the drab room. On the opposite wall were pictures of Chinese leaders. But what caught his attention was the crimson five-starred Chinese flag. He remembered that the large star in the left-hand corner represented the Communist party, while the small stars underneath it represented the people. Safe under the party.

Jeff shivered.

"My name is Captain Hu," the man said when they were all seated. "I'm part of the police force." He looked closely at each one of them. "It's very important that you answer my questions honestly. If you cooperate, everything will go well with you."

Jeff nodded, forcing a smile.

"What is the purpose of this trip, young man?"

Jeff was startled. Captain Hu was speaking to him. "We've...we've come to film our American bike team. We're members of a media club called the Reel Kids Adventure Club."

"Is your group religious?" Captain Hu asked.

Jeff paused for a moment, wanting to respond wisely.

Just then, Warren started to speak. Captain Hu raised his hands in anger. "I'm not talking to you. I'm asking the boy. What is your answer?"

Jeff trembled inside, but he knew he had to tell the truth. "Yes, our team believes in God and lives according to His principles." Jeff felt good about his answer. Captain Hu wanted an honest answer, and he got it.

"Do you know Thomas Johnson?" Captain Hu asked.

Jeff was stunned. Casting a quick glance at Mike, he struggled for words.

"Don't look at him," the captain ordered. "I'm asking you. Only look at me."

Jeff wished he could disappear. He knew he was trapped now. "Sir," he said slowly, "I don't know him personally. But I do know that Mr. Johnson is from America and teaches at Beijing University."

Captain Hu pulled a piece of paper out of his pocket. He placed it in Jeff's face. "Have you seen this before?"

Jeff couldn't believe his eyes. It was the fax Mike had sent. Cold anxiety filled his whole being.

Jeff forced himself to look up at Captain Hu. "We sent that."

Captain Hu became angry. "In this fax, you mention your need for translators to fulfill your mission."

Captain Hu paused. For a tense moment, silence filled the air.

"What is this mission you spoke of?"

Jeff lowered his head, feeling at a loss for words.

"Is your mission to share about your God?" Captain Hu stared scornfully at the others.

Jeff glanced at Mindy out of the corner of his eye. He couldn't remember when she had looked so frozen in fear. So terrified.

"Answer me!" Captain Hu demanded impatiently.

Jeff let out a gasp of air. He felt boldness rise up within him. "We are a media club," he said, "and we also believe in God."

Captain Hu laughed—a laughter mixed with anger. "And are you going to tell others about this God?"

Jeff took a deep breath. "I'll be honest with you, sir. We're not ashamed to talk to people about God.

Besides, your government allows for a Christian church, doesn't it?"

Captain Hu rolled his eyes in anger. "Our leaders wiped out Christianity in the Cultural Revolution. We still find traces here and there. But it's because of people like you who come here on so-called missions. Other nations in the world have been tricked by your false ideas. But that will never happen here, as long as I have anything to say about it."

Jeff didn't even dare move. He just listened, wondering what Captain Hu's real intentions were.

Captain Hu eyed each piece of luggage. "Open your backpacks and suitcases. Please remove each item."

Without looking at each other, the team lifted their bags onto the table. Slowly, Jeff pulled out his clothes, followed by candy, a hair brush, and all his other personal items. Reluctantly, he lifted out a pack of literature written in Mandarin and set it on the table.

Jeff hesitated.

Captain Hu raised his eyebrows. "I said every item."

His hands trembling, Jeff pulled out the hidden New Testaments until his bag was empty. He tried to appear calm as he waited for the expected response.

Captain Hu scowled as each team member placed a pile of Bibles on the old wooden table. Then he turned to Mindy. "What's a nice girl like you doing smuggling Bibles? Don't you know I can put you in jail for this?"

Mindy looked wide-eyed at Jeff, her face pale. He cast her a confused glance.

"Nice camera," Captain Hu huffed, turning his attention to K.J. "I could use something like that."

K.J. looked up, gripping the camera tightly. "Sir, please don't take it. We're a media club."

Tension hung in the room like a thick fog.

"I'll be back in a minute," Captain Hu snorted, ignoring K.J. "I must confer with some of my officers about your fate. Please remain here, and don't touch a thing." To make sure they obeyed, he placed a guard inside the room.

Jeff leaned closer to Mike. "Do you think Thomas will be in big trouble? And the translators?"

"No names were mentioned in the fax. The Chinese government is pretty easy on Americans. I think they're just trying to scare us—especially Captain Hu, for whatever reason."

Mindy sighed. "It's working."

"How did they get that fax?" K.J. asked.

"We were pretty desperate," Mike said thoughtfully. "I tried to be careful, but maybe we shouldn't have sent it." He kept his voice low. "There are lots of informers in China. Someone at the college who knows about what Thomas does must have spotted it and reported it."

"Maybe we shouldn't have brought Bibles in. Is smuggling wrong?"

Warren's eyes brightened. "Mindy, the most loving thing a believer can do is bring the Word of God to a nation that doesn't know God. If we don't, that nation will perish in darkness. God's Word brings light to the darkest places."

Mindy smiled. "You're right. In preparing for this trip, I was shocked to find out how scarce the

Bible is in China. A few years ago, one Bible among twenty or thirty people was common. I even read about a village with only one Bible for more than one thousand Christians. They copy it over and over and pass it around. The believers spend hours memorizing it."

The other team members grinned at each other. Mindy was a great researcher, and she loved to share what she learned. Happily, she went on.

"The average American has at least three or four Bibles. These Chinese Christians would give everything for a few pages."

"Wow," K.J. said in astonishment. "Talk about a new perspective. I'm going to treasure my Bible like never before."

Warren nodded, knowing God had established a wonderful truth in young hearts.

Mindy looked at Mike, her smile fading. "What do you think of Captain Hu?"

"I can't figure him out," Mike said. "I've been across this border many times. I've never dealt with anyone so harsh. It's like he's got some ax to grind. I know one thing—if we get out of here, he's really going to keep an eye on us."

The team sat in silence, pondering Mike's words.

When Captain Hu returned, he had a smug look on his face. "I've talked to my officers. We're going to keep you, as you Americans say, on a short leash."

"Does that mean we're free to go?" Jeff asked.

"It means you can still do your little bike trip, but we'll be watching your every move."

"And what does that mean?"

"Let me make it clear. It means that you're forbidden to give out Bibles or any other literature.

And you're forbidden to talk to anyone about your God along the road."

Captain Hu looked at them sternly. "I guess you could say that any road you travel is a forbidden road."

Chapter 5

Little Black Books

Jeff stared bleakly at Captain Hu. "We didn't come here to cause trouble, sir. We want to be a blessing to the Chinese people."

"I'm warning you," the captain said sternly. "I'm personally making sure you're watched. You can pick up your Bibles and other propaganda when you leave. If it were up to me, I'd throw everything in the trash pile." His eyes narrowed. "It's teaching like this that has hindered the great ideals of Karl Marx from being completely fulfilled."

Captain Hu turned to K.J. "You're lucky I'm not taking your camera. But if I find you talking about your God, I will. We don't need your God in our land. We will build a great nation without any Western ideas."

K.J. turned red as he listened to the captain scold him.

"Now put your clothes and the rest of your things back in your bags and get out of here."

The team hurriedly packed their bags. When they were outside the room, everyone let out a huge gasp of relief, happy to lose themselves in the large crowd of travelers. If the situation weren't so serious, Jeff would have laughed to see how tightly K.J. was holding onto his camera equipment.

Mike turned to the others. "We need to catch a taxi to the youth hostel." He saw the confused look on K.J.'s face. "It's like a hotel. That's where we'll meet Thomas and the others."

Before long, the team bounced along in a taxi, exhausted from the stressful day. Jeff strained to take in each passing scene. He had waited a long time to see Beijing, the famous capital of China. Now he would have to wait until morning.

"Do you think they've gotten to Thomas yet?" he asked Mike.

"We'll see, won't we?"

K.J. got angry. "Boy, I'd like to have punched that guy in the nose."

"I'm glad you didn't," Mindy said. "I hear Chinese prisons are pretty bad. Rats and everything."

"Well, I'm glad I didn't punch him either."

"What can we do now?" Jeff asked. "We don't have any materials left. I wanted to film us passing out literature."

Mike smiled. "All we have left are our voices."

"Captain Hu said we're forbidden to do anything, though—even share. What shall we do about that?"

Warren was ready to answer. "We'll be very careful," he said, looking over his shoulder at Jeff. "But remember in the Book of Acts when the angry leaders told Peter and John they were forbidden to speak in Jesus' name?"

Everyone nodded.

"Well, Peter and John asked the leaders whether it was right to obey God or man. Then Peter and John called a big prayer meeting. God gave them boldness to speak in His name."

K.J grinned. "So it would have been worse to disobey God?"

"Right," Warren agreed. "But that doesn't mean we should disobey authorities. It's just that God puts a high value on His message being heard by those who don't know him."

"That's because it's the only truth to save mankind and help us live right," Mindy said. "I read somewhere that God's Word is like the repair manual that goes with a car. If you don't have the manual, you can't fix the car."

"And what we want to do is bring people the owner's manual," Jeff exclaimed, feeling a renewed enthusiasm for their mission.

"And God will make it possible," Warren said confidently. "Leaders have no right to keep the Word of God from the people."

"You know," Jeff said, "I've been doing a lot of thinking about China lately. One-fifth of all the people on earth are Chinese."

K.J. gave a wide-eyed grin. "Wow! As fast as the church is growing here, that means we'll probably be eating a lot of Chinese food in heaven. I'd love it. Egg rolls forever."

Mindy chuckled. "It means chopsticks, too, K.J. And I've seen you use those."

"I still can't wait to try the food here," K.J. insisted, pretending to be offended.

"I hate to tell you," Mindy said, "but I hear that food isn't that plentiful here."

Everyone laughed.

Before long, the taxi pulled up in front of the youth hostel.

"How much does it cost to stay here?" Jeff asked.

"About five dollars a night," Mike said. "A lot cheaper than the thirty dollars we paid at the YMCA."

Jeff looked over the apartment building, or flat as the British called it. "Nothing fancy about this place. I hear the city used to be so beautiful. What happened?"

"Wait till you see the rest of Beijing in the daylight. Since the Communist Revolution, the city looks like a row of dull, gray dominoes. Many cities in China look that way now."

As the team left the taxi, Mike suddenly dropped his bags. Running to the lighted entrance, he gave an American-looking man a big bear hug.

"This is Thomas," he said when the team had caught up. "We have lots to thank him for."

Thomas beamed, pumping each of their hands. "It's so nice to meet you. I have rooms reserved for you. Chen and Jinghau will meet us here in the morning."

Jeff smiled. Thomas might look distinguished in his dark pants and tie, but Jeff could tell already that this was a man with a lot of enthusiasm. His voice boomed, and his blue eyes were full of life.

The professor helped the team carry their bags inside and check into their rooms. He had arranged for Mindy to have a small room with a bunk bed and for the guys to stay together in a larger room with single beds. Looking around the room, Jeff was struck by the concrete floors, dull painted walls and old furniture. He guessed for five dollars one couldn't be picky. Besides, this would suit their needs just fine.

Since it was getting late, they all gathered right away in the large room. Captain Hu had not contacted Thomas yet, and Mike needed to bring him up to date on the airport interrogation. As Mike went over every detail, everyone relived the frightening experience.

"How long have you been teaching here?" Warren asked, when there was nothing more to tell about the interrogation.

Thomas smiled. "Five years. God called me to be a missionary years ago. It's very difficult to get into China long-term, and teaching is one of the best ways."

"What if you get caught sharing the Gospel?" Mindy asked.

"The government has loosened up some. But it

gets very angry when you are aggressive in sharing your faith. Years ago, the government demanded that all churches and groups become one church called 'The Three Self Movement.' Though a political trick, it allowed for a Christian church, at least a very weak one. It's the house churches that are thriving."

Mindy listened carefully as Thomas went on.

"To stay here requires great wisdom in what and how I share. That's why I like to sponsor teams like yours."

"Do you think Captain Hu will put the heat on you now?" Jeff asked.

"You better believe it," Thomas said emphatically. "I'll have to lay low. He sounds like a pretty mean customer."

"He is," K.J. exclaimed. "He took our Bibles and literature with an almost evil passion. Do you know where we can get more?"

Thomas laughed. "It's not easy. I've given everything I have to other teams. I wish we could go to a Christian bookstore and buy Bibles, but there isn't one."

"Maybe someday," Mindy said. "I believe China will someday be a strong Christian nation and have lots of Bibles."

"Yes!" Thomas agreed passionately. "Now, why don't we go over the plan for your trip?"

"Good idea," Mike said. "Tomorrow, Warren and I need to rent bikes and a mini-van. We thought it would be great if Chen and Jinghau would take Jeff, K.J. and Mindy into Beijing for a tour of the Forbidden City and Tiananmen Square."

Mike looked at some notes. "We plan to bike to the Great Wall on Thursday and Friday. We'll stop at villages to share with people and, of course, film along the way."

"What route are you taking back?" Thomas asked.

"We want to loop through the Shanxi province for a couple days and arrive back in Beijing next Monday morning."

"I'm tired just thinking about it," Mindy said. "I'm going to bed."

"Sounds good to me," Jeff said, yawning. "I'm exhausted."

K.J. grinned. "I'm staying up a while. I want this equipment in perfect working order. I don't want to miss a thing."

Thomas smiled at K.J.'s enthusiasm. "I am so glad your team came. Just make sure you don't film any military facilities—and stay out of restricted zones."

"What's a restricted zone?" K.J. asked. "Is that like the Forbidden City?"

Mike and Thomas laughed.

"No," Mike said. "The Forbidden City is now open to the public. Restricted zones are off limits to foreigners."

K.J. looked confused.

"In certain provinces," Thomas explained, "there are cities, villages and countryside that can't be traveled in. If you're caught off the main highway in those zones, there will be trouble."

Jeff rubbed his tired eyes and reached for his Bible, feeling lucky he still had his own. Hot shafts of sunshine had woken him this morning. He had been anxious for the day to start, so he'd gotten up and dressed.

Still groggy, he lay back down on his bed and opened to his daily devotions. With bleary eyes, he read Psalm 119. Every verse spoke of the power of God's Word. Everything the club had discussed the night before was coming alive in the Bible.

Jeff read on with astonishment, knowing God was speaking to him. The Psalmist wrote about how he couldn't live without God's Word—his guide, teacher and rock.

Sorrow filled Jeff's heart when he thought of the Bibles that had been taken from them. He knew they had lost life lines for saving scores of people drowning in darkness.

Jeff fought discouragement. He prayed for thousands of new Bibles. His heart almost burst thinking about the potential. Feeling embarrassed by the tears in his eyes, he peeked over at the others. They were sound asleep. Then he saw Warren open his eyes.

"Good morning," Jeff whispered. "I'm really excited about today."

Warren flopped sleepily out of bed, while Mike and K.J. aroused slowly.

"Let's get some breakfast," Jeff whispered.

"Let me get dressed first," Warren grunted.

"Okay. I'll go for a little walk."

Walking out the door, Jeff spotted Mindy coming out of her room.

"Good morning," Mindy chirped. "Where are you going?"

Jeff was about to answer when he noticed two men hurrying out of the room next to his. Remembering all the Europeans they had seen at the airport, he figured they were tourists. Jeff decided to greet them.

"Good morning," he said. "Do you know a good place to get breakfast around here?"

The older man smiled. "Next door is good. We just ate there. We're leaving today. Did you just arrive?"

Quickly, Jeff told them about their bike trip. After a few minutes, he felt strongly that he should tell them they were Christians.

The men grinned at each other.

"What's wrong?" Mindy asked.

The younger man laughed. "How would you like some little black books?"

Chapter 6

Tiananmen Square

Jeff couldn't believe his ears. He stared first at Mindy, then at the men. He knew what they were talking about.

He moved closer so he could speak quietly. "We had our stuff taken at the airport. I was just praying for Bibles."

The men winked at each other.

"We're Americans living in Hong Kong," the younger man explained. "We take Bibles in from time to time."

Jeff's jaw dropped. The man went on.

"A few days ago, the Lord directed us to fill our

backpacks and bring them in. We didn't know why. We just obeyed."

"I'm...I'm in shock," Jeff stammered. "We come along while you guys are just leaving. This is amazing."

Jeff and Mindy helped the men put the Bibles in Mindy's room. There were at least four dozen little black New Testaments written in Mandarin, and a new supply of tracts and literature. Jeff was beside himself.

Before the men left, Jeff introduced them to the others. When they had gone, everyone looked at each other in utter disbelief. Jeff knew God was up to something.

After breakfast, Jeff looked at his watch. It was 8:30. Chen and Jinghau would be there soon. Everyone decided to head upstairs to their rooms for the few minutes before they came.

Suddenly, Jeff gulped in fear. Looking near the reception desk, he rubbed his eyes. There was one of Captain Hu's men, staring right at them. Jeff remembered him from the airport. A short, stocky man in uniform.

Jeff's heart gave a sudden leap, drumming wildly inside his chest. He felt trapped. Questions raced through his mind. He wondered if Captain Hu had sent the men with the Bibles as a set up. Was this his trap to throw them in jail?

Jeff looked at Warren.

"Walk by fast. Don't look his way," Warren whispered firmly.

About to explode, Jeff tried to calm his rising fear. Any moment they would find out if they had been set up.

Rapidly, Jeff walked past the man, feeling his cold stare. The others followed. Once inside the stairway, Jeff turned to Mike and Warren.

"What do we do now? If they find those Bibles, we're cooked ducks."

K.J. managed a grin. "Yeah. Peking ducks. Peking was the name of Beijing before, you know."

"Cute," Mindy hissed. "But not very funny right now."

"Where did you put the Bibles?" Thomas asked, climbing the stairs.

"Under Mindy's bed," Jeff whispered.

"Let's hope that guy doesn't search the rooms," Mike said.

Jeff frowned. "How can we get them out of here with him hanging around?"

"I don't know," Thomas admitted. "It's really strange that a captain is taking this much interest in you."

"Maybe it's just a coincidence that he's here," Warren replied hopefully.

"We'll know soon enough," Mindy said.

"Let's have a prayer meeting in our room," Jeff suggested.

Warren nodded. "Good idea. Let's stay away from Mindy's room until he leaves."

Almost as soon as they went in, they heard a loud knock. Jeff almost jumped out of his skin.

"Do you think it's him?" Mindy whispered.

"We'll find out," K.J. said, heading for the door.

Slowly, he opened it. Jeff wanted to close his eyes. Then K.J. let out a sigh of relief.

It was Chen and Jinghau.

Everyone breathed easier.

"Boy, are we glad to see you," Thomas said, rising to welcome them.

After everyone was introduced, Mike briefed the newcomers about the man in the lobby and the airport interrogation with Captain Hu.

Jeff studied Chen and Jinghau. Both were dressed in black pants and white T-shirts. Other than that, the brother and sister didn't look alike. Chen was rather short, with dark eyes and an engaging, warm smile. Jinghau was taller. Her big eyes, perfect skin, and long black hair added to her beauty.

Jinghau smiled. "We're very glad to translate for you. We love Jesus with all our hearts. We always pray for opportunities to share our faith."

K.J. grinned at her, turning slightly red. "Can I ask you two a question?"

They both nodded yes.

"Do you guys know how to ride bikes?"

The team laughed. Jinghau looked confused, but she smiled anyway, showing her dimples. "Chinese people ride really well. You'll see thousands of bikes around here. They're quite different from the ones we'll be using. Mountain bikes are much easier to ride."

K.J. let out a gasp of air. "Good. I don't want anybody else to get hurt on this trip."

"Are you ready to go on a tour?" Chen asked.

"As long as Captain Hu's men don't go with us," Mindy laughed.

Chen and Jinghau smiled.

"We're glad to hear you're university students," Warren said from his perch on one of the beds. "Can you tell us a little about yourselves?"

Jinghau looked embarrassed.

Chen spoke up. "We know you have so many questions. You can ask anything you like. We want to tell you all about life in China."

Mindy's eyes lit up. "That would be great."

"We are very privileged to be in university," Chen explained. "It is much different than in America. Thousands of students apply to go, but you have to work very hard to pass entry exams. If you fail, it's back to the farm. We can get a better job if we work hard—very hard. Life is not easy on campus. That's why we're glad to be with you this week."

"We're so blessed to have you," Jeff said.

For the next few minutes, everyone shared with each other. Jeff knew God was drawing the team closer together.

An hour later, Jeff, Mindy and K.J. followed their new friends downstairs. Warren and Mike had just left to get the bikes and van with Thomas. Downstairs, Jeff carefully scanned the reception area. The man who had been watching them was gone.

"I guess those guys were for real. I thought for sure we were set up."

Chen grinned. "Forget about that for now. We want to show you around the city. And treat you to a good lunch."

K.J. smiled. "Now you're talking."

"Let's catch a taxi to Tiananmen Square," Jinghau suggested. "There's lots to learn about China's history there."

Jeff couldn't wait. Though it was already getting hot, he was anxious to see the city.

K.J. lifted up his camera bag. "I'm ready to film. Just give me the word."

Jeff was fascinated by the sights he saw from the taxi window. "Those buildings sure are close together," he commented.

Chen nodded. "Since Chairman Mao Zedong established the People's Republic in 1949, everything has changed."

"How's that?" Jeff asked.

"You'll see," Chen said.

"Look at all those bikes," K.J. cried, as they got closer to the city. "And listen to those ringing bicycle bells."

"I told you," Jinghau laughed. "Beijing is a city of bicycles. People are too poor to own cars."

Jeff smiled. Chen and Jinghau were going to make great additions to the team. He was thankful they were so willing to share about their country. He peered out at the rows of gray apartment buildings. Five-story buildings were everywhere. They really did look like gray dominoes, just as Mike had said.

At the next stoplight, Jinghau pointed to some old brick buildings. "Here is an old residential district. This is what China used to look like a hundred years ago. Lots of traditional single-story brick houses with U-shaped courtyards."

Looking closer, Jeff saw a courtyard strung with clotheslines bowed down by hanging white shirts and baggy blue trousers. All around were earthen jars, pots of flowers, brooms, and clay jars crammed in the nooks and crannies of the courtyard.

Jinghau looked sad. "Now everything is dull and plain."

As they drove on, Jeff noticed a field of mud on the edge of a large construction project. A huge crane swung to lift a cement bucket toward a brick wall jutting up from a swatch of earth bordered by roadways.

"This is the last trace of a forty-foot wall that encircled the city," Jinghau volunteered. "It was a work of beauty."

Jeff turned to watch the crumbled wall disappear behind them. Worn and gap-toothed, what was left was supported by dark, sinewy timbers exposed here and there. Stacks of new burnt orange bricks and charcoal gray blocks were piled around the ruin.

"Why did they ruin everything?" Mindy asked.

Chen smiled when he saw that Mindy had her pencil ready to take notes. "Communism's goal was to bring equality to all," he explained. "But it tries to accomplish this without God and always sacrifices individual rights for the supposed good of the community. It cares nothing for the parts, only the whole. Chairman Mao wanted total change. Everybody had to dress the same, live the same and own the same. But it didn't work."

"I still don't get it," Mindy said.

"Nobody gets it," Chen said. "We are people like everyone else. When our dreams, goals and individual desires are taken away, it makes us feel worthless and disrespected. It's hard to make a strong, productive community out of those kind of people. That's why Communism has failed and always will fail. It never reaches its goal of equality. Only control, oppression, and finally the people throw the godless system off."

Jinghau nodded. She and her brother had obviously thought about this a lot. "Chairman Mao's attempt to transform China set us back years. He tried to change things too fast. When Mao and his comrades declared China the People's Republic, he ordered his best architects to redesign the cities. With one wave of Mao's hand, he wiped out old scenes of graceful yellow tile roofs, emerald green tree tops and magnificent city walls. He wanted to see chimneys all over Beijing."

Jinghau paused a minute, wiping a tear from her eye. "He got his wish, didn't he?"

"Why chimneys?" K.J. asked.

"It meant factories, which meant greater production. But what it really meant was the slavery of a billion people. Anyone who challenged Chairman Mao was shot or sent to prison. He called the revolution the People's Movement."

Jeff felt angry listening to the sad history.

"So why did the people follow him in the first place?" K.J. asked.

Chen smiled as if K.J. had asked the perfect question. "China had been isolated from the modern world for so long that the Chinese people were not prepared for the crippling influence of the Western nations. After years of being ruled by an emperor, the attempt to establish democracy and a republic was not working well. By the time Mao came along, the people were disillusioned with the present government, and the stage was set for a dramatic revolutionary change."

"Go on," Mindy said, scribbling notes. "This is interesting."

"Linked with that," Chen said sadly, "the Chinese people always made the ruler of China the 'Son of Heaven' and thought him superior to all the rest of earth's rulers. They thought the mantle of heaven had fallen on him. Besides that, the Chinese have always given up individual rights for loyalty to the clan. That's why they obediently followed emperors for hundreds of years. To them, Mao was about to become like a god. He would deliver them from their oppressive and greedy landowners and solve the problems of all the peasants."

"But he didn't," K.J. cried.

"No Communist leader has or will," Jinghau said pointedly. "China made the mistake of other nations in the past century. It bought the lie."

Jeff leaned back on his seat. "I'm glad Communism is dying around the world. It's done more to stifle freedom and kill innocent people than any other movement."

Jinghau nodded sadly. "In China, it's alive outwardly. The leaders and the army are still in control. But we're hopeful that Communism will fall apart like it did in Russia and other places. It's doomed because it believes in man alone and doesn't recognize God."

Jeff painfully remembered the persecution people had suffered worldwide since 1917 because of Communism. Especially in China.

Arriving at Tiananmen Square, Jeff pondered the painful history of this thirty-four-acre square. He remembered the university students' attempt to overthrow Communism.

Jinghau pointed straight ahead. "China's destiny has been wrapped up in this little piece of land, in these few acres. Over there is the Gate of Heavenly Peace. I'll tell you more about it as we get closer."

K.J. shaded his eyes and looked around. "I'll bet Captain Hu is watching us somewhere."

"I hope not," Mindy shuddered. "That guy gives me the creeps."

"I don't believe it," K.J. exclaimed. "There's a Kentucky Fried Chicken place over there. Can we get some lunch?"

Everyone laughed.

Mindy rolled her eyes. "What happened to your love for Chinese food?" She grinned at K.J., then turned serious. "In my research, I studied this square a lot. I'll try to remember some things as we go."

Jeff nodded. He remembered learning a little bit about the horrible events of 1989 in school. "If I remember right," he said, "the university students tried to break the back of Communism, especially after many other Communist nations had fallen."

"That's right," Jinghau said.

"Let me tell you some stuff," Mindy grinned, excited to share her research. "Like Jinghau already showed us, over there is the Gate of Heavenly Peace. Chairman Mao climbed it in 1949 to proclaim the New People's Republic of China. This was after fighting the old government of Chiang Kai-shek for years."

"Pretty good, Mindy," Chen smiled. "I'm impressed."

"Tiananmen means heavenly peace," Jinghau said. "The gate is also called the Tiananmen Gate. It guards the southern approach to the former imperial palace. The people believed that 'emperor power' radiated out across the courtyards and palace to the countryside. Of the five bridges leading to the gate, only the emperor could cross the middle one. After the revolution, Chairman Mao put up an immense color portrait of himself there. It was here in the square that he reviewed the Red Guards, a million or more strong army of young people who had enlisted in his cause."

"Did Chairman Mao mean well in the beginning?" K.J. asked.

Jinghau rolled her eyes. "Most revolutionaries start out okay. Then they embrace Communism so totally, they completely forget about the individual and become tyrants who control and enslave the people. Chairman Mao was no different. After he died in 1976, the truth came out. It resulted in his wife and three other leaders being arrested. They were called the Gang of Four."

"How did he get into power?" K.J. asked.

"He led a peasant army on what was called 'the

long march' in 1939. After winning, he became a hero and chairman of the Communist party. Putting his teachings in a little red book, he made it the bible of China. Then he wiped out the real Bible, the church and all freedoms. People fanatically followed him because they thought he would bring freedom. Instead, he brought poverty, persecution and death."

When his sister had finished, Chen pointed straight ahead. "We're nearing the Forbidden City. It's where all of China's emperors used to live. You'll love the rust-colored pagodas with their red tile roofs. They were built by human hands but designed to blend right into the architecture of nature."

"I remember seeing an amazing movie about China called *The Last Emperor*," Jeff cried. "I can't believe I'm here."

Mindy grinned. "The Last Emperor was crowned at age three in 1908. He was called the Son of Heaven and the Lord of Ten Thousand Years."

"He didn't make ten thousand, did he?" K.J. laughed.

"No," Mindy said. "He hardly left the Forbidden City, where hundreds served him. It took him a while to discover that he had lost his power. After years in prison, the Last Emperor died in 1957."

Slowly, they walked along the Avenue of Eternal Peace. Jeff knew it was another name revealing the hopes of the Chinese people. Nearing a canopy of beautiful sycamore trees fringing the wall of the ancient Forbidden City, Jeff saw the vastness of the square stretching away from him like a huge lake. Stepping onto the checkerboard of cement stones, his heart raced. He couldn't believe he was actually in Tiananmen Square.

Looking toward the five marble bridges leading to the Gate of Heavenly Peace, he realized the gate was the only entrance to the Forbidden City—the only way through the thick, towering walls that once surrounded the Forbidden City and Beijing, as well as many other Chinese towns and cities.

Jeff stared at the huge gate Mao had climbed. Over 110-feet high, it had five passages through it. He saw the wooden tower with a double roof of glazed tile. The five marble bridges led inside.

As they entered the Forbidden City, Mindy's eyes danced with excitement. "Over there are the beautiful courtyards, palaces and halls where the emperors lived and entertained their guests for many, many years."

K.J. had his camcorder rolling. Jeff stood in awe, imagining all the emperors who had lived there. For the next few hours, the team studied all the sights and even ate fried chicken.

On the way out, K.J. stopped. "Mike wants us to get an interview right here."

"Okay," Jeff agreed. "Let's have Chen and Jinghau give a fast summary of Tiananmen Square and hope the tape inspires kids to come back here to pray and share their faith."

K.J. started the camera rolling. Jeff smiled right into the lens. "Today we're standing in front of the famous Tiananmen Gate. Mindy Caldwell is with me, as well as Chen and Jinghau Lee. We've just finished a tour of the Forbidden City."

Jeff turned to Mindy. "Mindy, please describe what you see."

Mindy spoke in a clear, bold voice, "Beijing is the capital of China. I'm standing in one of the most interesting squares we could ever visit.

"As you can see, my back is to the Tiananmen Gate. Directly to my right and on the west side of the square is the Great Hall of the People. The National People's Congress sits here when it is in session. Heads of state are also entertained here."

Mindy pointed to her left. "Over here to the east is the Museum of Chinese Revolution and Chinese History. Straight ahead is the Monument to the People's Heroes, and directly behind is the Mao Zedong Memorial Hall. Chairman Mao's body is preserved here in a red-flag-draped crystal coffin."

Mindy went on for a few minutes. Finally, Jeff wrapped it up. "Thanks, Mindy." He turned to Chen and Jinghau. "Please give us some more history of this square."

Chen was the first to speak up. "It was here that the famous May 4th movement began in 1919. It inspired a whole generation of people to try to get rid of their corrupt government. Years later, it ended in the Communist Revolution. It was also here that Chairman Mao assembled millions of recruits to join his People's Liberation Army."

"What happened in 1989?" Jeff asked.

Jinghau looked solemnly into the camera. "On June 4, 1989, over one million university students and others gathered here to protest Communist rule. They erected a goddess of democracy out of plaster, like America's Statue of Liberty. Students believed it was time for heaven to appoint another son."

"What happened?" Jeff asked.

Jinghau wiped away a tear. "As most of the world knows, thousands of university students were gunned down by tanks and guns in cold blood. Suddenly, the freedom revolution was crushed."

Jeff knew it was time to finish. He could almost picture the nightmarish scenes he had seen on video at school. He gathered his thoughts. "What can people pray about?"

"Pray that the true Son of Heaven, the Son of God, will rule here."

Jeff smiled and was about to conclude the segment. Suddenly, his eyes were drawn across the square. A group of policemen was headed their way.

Captain Hu walked rapidly in the lead.

Chapter 7

Getting Started

Immediately, Jeff finished the interview. His heart raced as he looked into the camera and made his final plea to the future viewers. "Please pray that freedom will come to this square again."

K.J. put down his camera. Jeff worried that Chen and Jinghau would be in trouble. He wanted to run, but he knew it was too late. The men stared right at them. The team would have to face them.

"Just think of our mission," Jeff whispered to the others.

Captain Hu strode up. His men stopped a few feet behind. "So how's your film coming?" he asked sarcastically.

Jeff smiled. "Fine."

"Who are your friends?"

"These are our Chinese guides."

"Yes," Captain Hu said. "I'm aware of them."

Everyone remained silent. Jeff didn't bat an eye.

Captain Hu looked back to one of his men. "This is Mr. Wan Lee. He has been assigned by me to keep an eye on you."

Mr. Lee nodded, his face showing no emotion.

Jeff studied the tall Chinese man. He had a rounded face and dark mustache and was muscular enough to noticeably fill out his uniform. And if his muscles weren't enough, Jeff noted he also wore a gun.

Captain Hu looked at K.J.'s camera. "Maybe I should view your video."

K.J. took a slight step back.

Captain Hu laughed. "Don't worry," he said. "I wouldn't waste my time. But Mr. Lee will be checking everything you shoot."

Jeff felt weak.

Captain Hu laughed again. "If you'll excuse me, I must be going. I have business to tend to. But remember my warning."

When Captain Hu had gone, Jeff looked up into the eyes of Mr. Lee. They were expressionless. Mr. Lee looked at the camera. Reluctantly, K.J. handed it to him. After a few minutes, Mr. Lee handed it back.

"You really believe all this religious stuff," Mr. Lee said, grinning in amusement at what he thought was foolishness.

"Yes," Jeff replied, unashamed.

"My job is to make sure you don't spread it around.

If I catch you, I'll take away your video equipment."

The team nodded their understanding, and Mr. Lee hurried off with another officer.

Jeff gasped in relief. "That was a close call. Let's get out of here."

When the taxi pulled up to the youth hostel, Warren and Mike were out front, surrounded by mountain bikes. Looking around, Jeff spotted the light blue van that they must have rented. The excitement in the taxi was almost tangible.

Mindy jumped out first. "Where's my bike?"

"Probably the pink one," K.J. teased. "With the lavender flowers."

"Cool it," Mindy blurted. "There's none like that." She studied them. "Here. This must be mine. It's the one without the boy bar going across."

Everyone laughed.

"How was your day?" Warren asked. "Did Chen and Jinghau go on home?"

Jeff nodded, then filled them in. Especially about Captain Hu's visit and Mr. Lee.

"How are we going to get the Bibles out of the room?" K.J. asked. "I'm sure we're being watched."

"Yeah," Mindy added. "And where are we going to keep them?"

Warren nodded. "We've thought about that all day. We're going to have to get up really early. Around 4:30. Hopefully Captain Hu and Mr. Lee sleep a little."

"And what if they don't?" Mindy asked.

"We'll have to take that chance," Warren said firmly.

"Where are we going to keep them?" Mindy pressed.

"In the van, in a panel near the spare tire."

Mindy's eyes grew as big as saucers. K.J.'s, too.

"This could be a good movie."

"Yeah," Mindy said. "A real spine-tingling thriller."

"Let's not worry now," Warren replied. "Let's find something to eat and get to bed early."

Early Thursday morning, darkness still had its grip on the land. It was four o'clock when the team started packing up. Chen and Jinghau had just arrived.

Jeff stared at the backpacks holding the Bibles. He offered up a quick prayer for God's protection.

"What shall we load first?" he asked.

"The bikes," Mike replied. "Unchain them and put them in the van."

"Which way are we going?" K.J. asked, as they went downstairs and out into the darkness.

Mike pointed north. "We'll catch a taxi to Chiangpin Road. It's the road we'll take to Badaling, where we'll view the Great Wall."

"Cool," K.J. said. "How far is it to Badaling?"

Mindy grinned with pride. "About forty miles."

"That's a long way," K.J. said. "I hear it's an uphill ride for the last few miles. Are we doing it all today?"

Warren laughed. Chen and Jinghau giggled.

"No, K.J. This isn't the Olympics. We're going to break it up into a two-day journey. We want to take time to visit some of the villages along the way. And there are quite a few of them—almost side to side."

"Good," K.J. groaned. "I don't want to rush through this. I want to do a lot of filming."

"Besides," Mike said. "China's road systems aren't the best. Especially this one. It will be dusty, and there's lots of gravel and potholes along the way. You won't believe the number of bikes that will be sharing the road with us—bikes and tourist buses heading to the Great Wall and over-loaded trucks delivering supplies to the villages. We'll need to take our time."

K.J. nodded slowly.

"It's time to take the Bibles," Warren said, when they were back in their room.

"Can we say a quick prayer?" Jeff asked.

Everyone bowed their head, as Warren nodded for Jeff to begin.

"Father, thanks for watching over us. Please help get Your Word to the right people and especially to the van."

Everyone added their amen.

Jeff reached for one of the backpacks. He walked slowly down the steps. Looking every direction he could, he saw no one. Stepping outside, he headed cautiously to the van, conscious of Mindy behind him carrying the other pack.

Suddenly, a man started walking toward them. Jeff felt his blood pressure rise.

"What shall we do now, Mindy?"

"Keep walking," Mindy whispered.

The stranger came closer and closer. Darkness hid his face. The man stopped abruptly, speaking in Mandarin. He sounded angry. Jeff stood still, frozen in panic.

Just then, Chen came out of the building.

"What's he trying to say?" Jeff asked tensely.

Chen listened carefully. "He wants your room key."

Jeff smiled in relief. "Tell him we'll return it shortly."

Mindy had turned pale white. Now she was giggling. "I can't take too much more of this."

Chen laughed. Missing the whole episode, Mike and Warren came outside. They carefully hid the Bibles inside the van.

Pulling up in the taxi to Chiangpin Road, everyone was excited to get going. The taxi unloaded its passengers along a row of dry trees. Jeff watched the team run up to the van, where he had ridden with Warren.

Quickly, he got out. "Okay, you guys. We've waited a long time for this moment. Let's get those bicycles out."

K.J. was excited, even for K.J. With the camera running, he yelled out, "let's do an interview. With the sun coming up, it'll be awesome."

For the next few minutes, Jeff questioned Mike about the details of the trip.

By that time, everyone was ready. Jeff was glad Warren was driving the van. It would give the team members a rest at times and provide needed storage. Everyone would carry only a small bag on the luggage rack.

Slinging a leg over his blue, 26-inch mountain bike, Jeff sat down on the seat. All the bikes were twelve speeds, equipped with toe-clip straps for power riding. Safety equipment like pedal reflectors and night lights made him feel safer for night riding. Even air pumps and racks for light luggage were included.

Mike required everyone to wear safety helmets, and they all wore T-shirts and shorts to stay cool. Jeff was glad for the water bottle clipped to his bike. July was the hottest and most humid month of the year in this area.

Finally, the team headed out. Pedaling down the road, they passed Chinese men and women carrying supplies on much slower bikes. Jeff couldn't believe they had actually begun. His legs felt strong, ready to ride. He grinned at K.J., who rode beside him. Up ahead, Mike and Chen rode together, while Jinghau stayed with Mindy. They had teased Warren about having the easy job of driving, but Jeff knew their leader would rather be out on the road with the rest of the team. Besides, it could be difficult to keep the van with the team in all the traffic.

"I can see villages for miles," K.J. yelled.

"And bikes," Mike laughed.

"And trucks," Mindy groaned. "Boy, it's dusty. How far are we going to go?"

"About ten kilometers."

"How much is a kilometer?" Mindy asked.

"About two-thirds of a mile."

"Good. I was hoping it wasn't more."

"Come on, Mindy," K.J. teased. "We're just getting started."

Viewing the beautiful countryside through the dust stirred up by the road, Jeff was filled with wonder. The Reel Kids Club was at last biking through China!

He noticed the rice patties terracing up the small hills and remembered that Mindy had explained that this was to allow good irrigation. She reported that even though much of the land was unsuitable for farming, over eighty percent of the people were involved in agriculture.

With growing anticipation, Jeff took in the passing scenes. It was people like the men and women he now saw working in the fields that they wanted to share the Gospel with.

"We'll stop at some village not too far from here," Mike hollered, when they had been riding for several hours.

Jeff looked back to see a red-faced Mindy. Huffing and puffing along, she was doing fine. He realized he was probably red-faced too.

Jeff laughed to himself, listening to the sound of horns honking from trucks and bikes. It was quite a scene. After a while, Mike slowed to a stop. Everyone pulled in behind him, motioning Warren to pull over.

"Let's take that narrow road," Mike said. "It's better to get off the main highway. When we get to the village, we'll break up into two teams. Jinghau will go with Jeff and Mindy, and Chen will go with us."

"Are we going to share with anybody about Jesus?" Mindy asked.

"If the right opportunity comes along, feel free to share. We may even give some Bibles out if we find the right person."

Jeff looked at his watch. It was almost ten o'clock. "When shall we meet back?"

"We can stay in the same area, but in case we get separated, let's plan to get some lunch around noon."

Mike took the lead again as they left the highway. Jeff was glad to get away from the dust and noise of the main road. Through the light dust flying about, he saw a solitary farmer wearing a sun hat. With a wooden plow balanced on his shoulder, the man was whacking the flanks of his water buffalo with a reed switch, as he and his beast plodded across the sunlit road toward a nearby paddy field.

Further along, Jeff saw a couple of drowsy young women in large-brimmed sun hats dozing behind metal tables scattered with warm sodas, crackers and cigarettes for sale.

As the team headed into the heart of the village, some of the Chinese stopped their work in the fields. Seeing the team on mountain bikes was a real show.

The smell of cooking fires filled the air. Jeff spotted two sidewalk merchants squatting under awnings, selling things from bamboo birdcages to car tires, dried mushrooms, vegetables and squawking ducks. Dogs, pigs and chickens ran wild, making a chorus of noises. Old men sat on tiny wood stools around low tables, playing cards and chess, smoking reed-thin pipes and chatting.

Jeff loved every minute of it. He looked further down the road, to where several unusual bikes were parked. Painted jet black, they were much bigger and heavier than the bikes the team was riding. They had only one speed, and all had little bells.

"Are all the bikes like these?" he asked.

Jinghau nodded. "Millions everywhere across China, all the same. Very few can afford mountain bikes."

"Look at those kids," Mindy cried, her heart melting at the sight.

Jeff spotted some young children playing near their mothers. Even with their tattered clothes and dirty faces, Jeff knew they were just like any kids, just like the kids at home.

Jinghau smiled. "It's easy to fall in love with our little ones."

"Let's talk to some of the people," Mindy said.

Jeff was proud of Mindy's boldness. Sometimes she was frightened at the beginning of trips, but she became bold once she was in the midst of the people. Jeff turned around to locate the others. He spotted K.J. filming as Mike, Warren and Chen talked with people. In fact, they had drawn a little crowd.

Jinghau moved close to some teenagers walking by.

"Can I talk to them?" Mindy asked.

"Sure," Jinghau said. "But be wise about the Bibles."

Jeff listened to Jinghau speak in Mandarin as Mindy told the group about the Reel Kids Adventure Club and of their trip to China. After a little while, Mindy found a young girl very interested. All the others listened closely, showing interest too.

"How old are you?" Mindy waited for Jinghau to translate.

"Seventeen."

Jeff thought the girl looked much younger.

"Have you heard about Jesus?" Mindy asked boldly. Jinghau translated.

"No."

Mindy was shocked. Tears came to her eyes as she shared the Gospel message. Jeff wasn't sure about all the kids, but he knew Mindy was getting through to some as she skillfully shared with them and answered their questions. They couldn't take their eyes off her.

"Can I pray with you?" Mindy asked the group.

A young Chinese girl wiped a tear from her eye. "I would like to pray," the girl said in broken English. "I want to know more about this God."

Jeff was surprised. Mike had told them that China was one of the easiest places in the world to share about Jesus. But Jeff thought this was too good to be true. He questioned the girl for a few moments, but found her to be very sincere.

Finally, Jeff, Mindy and Jinghau joined hands with their new friends. After leading them all in a prayer to accept Jesus into their hearts, they spent the next hour explaining more about God and His love.

Jeff forgot about the time. Suddenly, he looked at his watch. It was 12:30, and they were late.

Mindy turned to Jeff. "Can we give them Bibles?"

Jeff looked at Jinghau. She slowly nodded yes.

Racing to the van, Jeff reached for six Bibles. Returning, he gave them out. Then they said good-bye.

Mindy beamed like the noon sun. "I'm so happy! It's so much fun telling people about Jesus who have never heard. I hope they'll tell the whole village."

Jeff smiled. "Boy, I have never seen people so open to the Gospel. Mike told me that the people will flock to get literature."

"We better be careful," Mindy said.

Jeff nodded. Suddenly, his attention was drawn up the road. Dust was flying everywhere.

Chapter 8

Followed

Jeff stared straight at the red landrover speeding through the village.

"I hope it's not Captain Hu," Mindy cried.

Jeff shuddered. "I hope none of those kids tell on us."

He looked at the group of kids now walking in the direction of the oncoming landrover. A couple of them were reading the New Testaments.

"We're busted now," Jeff moaned.

"Don't panic," Jinghau said. "God is bigger."

Jeff looked for K.J.'s half of the team, but they were nowhere in sight.

Just as Jeff feared, the jeep pulled up alongside them. It was Mr. Lee. Jeff was relieved it wasn't Captain Hu himself, but Mr. Lee wasn't someone he wanted to see either.

Jinghau walked over to the officer's jeep. After greeting him, she talked with him in Mandarin. Finally, Jeff and Mindy dared to join her.

"What are you talking to the villagers about?" Mr. Lee asked angrily, speaking English now.

Jeff forced himself to smile. "We're answering their questions about life in America and about us."

"And what questions are those?" Mr. Lee asked.

"Any question they ask. We'll answer your questions too."

Mr. Lee laughed. "I don't need any answers from you." With that he sped away, leaving them in a cloud of choking dust.

Jeff was baffled. "What did he say to you earlier?"

"He warned us again. Captain Hu wants us to know he's still watching."

"Mr. Lee didn't see the Bibles, did he?" Mindy worried.

"I don't think so. I told you God is bigger."

Jeff smiled. "He sure is. Let's find the others and get some lunch."

The tiny restaurant was not what Jeff expected. He could see steam coming out of the cooking area and smell meat cooking. Old wooden tables were scattered about, covered with soiled and spotty tablecloths. Posters and pictures of China hung unevenly on the dirty walls. Glancing at the floor, Jeff saw bones from food people had eaten. He felt like he had suddenly gone back in time a hundred years.

K.J. looked around. "I'm not so sure I'm hungry anymore, unless there's a McDonald's near by. I wouldn't mind spending some *yuan* there."

Jinghau laughed aloud. "You almost said the name of our money right."

Everyone chuckled at K.J.

"We don't have many choices," Mike said. "If we want lunch, this is as good as it gets."

K.J.'s eyes widened. He pretended to frown at Jinghau. "Please order the best meal you can find."

Jinghau laughed again. "I will. But how many ways can you eat noodles? Besides," she smiled, "I think you'll like it."

When Chen and Jinghau had helped them order, everyone shared stories about the people they had met. Jeff was thrilled by the reports. Mike's team had shared and prayed with a family who then gave their lives to Jesus. They had heard about Jesus before, but only as a man of another religion.

The table buzzed with excitement when the food arrived. K.J. became a food inspector, carefully eyeing every bowl and plate set on the table. Jeff surveyed the table. Before him were two large bowls of rice and soup. Everything else was heaped on plates. One plate was piled with greens that looked like dandelions, and another with steaming hot noodles. Everyone had a medium-sized bowl and some chopsticks.

"How do you use these things?" K.J. blurted out.

Everyone laughed as K.J. tried to get the right grip on the chopsticks.

Chen and Jinghau filled their bowls. They knew the team wasn't used to the food. Mike smiled at them and filled his bowl.

"Can we get some sodas?" Mindy asked.

"This they have," Mike said, calling the server over.

Warren ate slowly, grinning at the others with each bite. After Jeff gulped down a big bite of the noodles, he grinned, crossing his eyes. Then he tried the tea, ignoring the grains floating in the water.

"Not bad," he said.

"We've got a ways to go today," Mike instructed. "You better eat. I didn't like this stuff at first, but I got used to it. You're going to need the energy for riding."

"Oh for some nice egg rolls," K.J. cried. "And sweet and sour chicken."

Just then, the server brought the sodas. K.J. took a quick drink.

"These are warm. Where's the ice?"

Chen and Jinghau laughed loudly along with Mike and Warren.

Mike put down his chopsticks. "This isn't California. They don't have ice here."

Everyone ate. "You know," Jeff offered, "this is really pretty good after all."

Mindy nodded in agreement. "I hope we don't get sick. The squatty potties that pass for restrooms here are not what I'd like to spend a lot of time in."

The heat was almost unbearable as they followed the main highway away from the beautiful flatlands and into the hills. Jeff figured it must be over a hundred degrees. His white T-shirt dripped with perspiration, already darkened with dust from the cream-colored soil that lined the road. Jeff noticed that the thatched-roof huts were made of the same soil. He remembered hearing that only the wealthy could afford tin roofs and better construction.

Pop! Hissss.

Startled, Jeff looked back at the other riders.

"Sounds like our first flat tire," Mike said. "Whose bike?"

Jeff looked at Mindy. Sure enough, her back tire was riding on the rim.

"Oh rats," Mindy cried. "I knew it was my bike." As she slowed down, she sighed. "Since it's so hot, I guess I needed a rest. Next time we do a bike trip, let's go at a cooler time."

K.J. nodded.

"Believe it or not," Mike said, "we'll need light jackets when we get into the higher mountains closer to the Great Wall."

Mindy grinned. That was hard to believe, all right.

Everyone pulled onto the gravel at the edge of the road. Mindy hopped off her bike. Mike got out his repair kit and went to work. Jeff looked down in surprise at all the tools he had: a crescent wrench, channel locks, screwdrivers, allen wrenches, vise grips, needle-nose pliers and a tire patch kit.

Mike smiled at Jeff. "I took a long bike trip once where we had over seventy flats. I needed all this stuff."

K.J. had volunteered earlier to help Mike repair equipment. After they started working, the others headed to the van to rest. Soon, Mike and K.J. strolled back to the van with the damaged tube.

"Boy," Mike said, "this is a big hole. A large nail must have got bent around inside the tire. A patch may not do it. I need a tube."

"Oh great," Mindy said. "There goes my bike trip."

"We can fix it," Mike said. "K.J. got some extra tubes the other day."

Just then, K.J.'s face turned beet red.

"What's wrong, K.J.?" Jeff asked. "You suddenly look sick."

K.J. hung his head. "I have a confession to make. I didn't get any tubes the other day. The first bike shop didn't have what we needed. I got so busy shopping that I forgot."

Mindy clenched her teeth, her face reddening. "See, you can't depend on K.J. for anything."

"Oh yeah?" K.J. said. "You were there. If you're the great detail person, why didn't you remind me?"

Mindy shifted uneasily, then walked away. Jeff knew she was steaming. He felt frustrated. After such a good morning, the tension was building.

K.J. threw a wrench on the ground and paced along the road. Jeff quickly walked over to him.

"K.J., you need to take responsibility for your mistake."

"Don't talk about mistakes. We've had nothing but trouble on this trip. It's not all my fault."

Jeff paused. "Take a moment to think about it. You'll see what I mean."

K.J. didn't blink an eye. Jeff knew his friend had been irresponsible. But he also knew the heat was getting to them all. He walked back to the van.

"Look," Mike said, "I can patch it, but it'll take a while. We need some drying time between patches. It's a big hole, and it got bigger as she rode."

"Why don't we pray first?" Warren suggested. "Let's not allow the enemy to drive us apart."

Mike nodded his encouragement.

Taking a deep breath, Jeff gathered the team. The tension was thick.

"Look," Jeff said. "We've got to stay together. Let's recognize the source of this attack."

No one responded. Finally, K.J. looked up.

"Okay," he said, calming a little. "I realize this is my fault. I'm sorry. It was pretty selfish of me. Will you all forgive me?"

Mindy tried to smile. "K.J., I'm sorry, too. My attitude stunk. Will you forgive me too?"

Jeff felt the tension disappear. For the next few minutes, they prayed while Mike worked on the tire. All at once, Jeff looked up. A Chinese woman was standing right next to them, her eyes fixed on their prayer circle.

Chapter 9

The China Cross

Jeff nodded to Chen, expecting him to say something. But the small lady looked right at Jeff.

"My name is Mary Woo. Can I talk to you?"

Jeff was shocked. She spoke good English. Looking around, he hoped Captain Hu wasn't behind this.

"Sure," he said, trying not to sound suspicious. "It's nice to meet you."

The others smiled at the woman. Though her face was wrinkled and sunburnt, and her back hunched, her eyes were very much alive. She wore the blue cotton tube-legged pants of a villager and a blue shirt with large white plastic buttons. Her steel gray hair was curiously fixed atop her head with a single large bobby pin.

"I live over there in that small farming village," she said, pointing. "When I saw you praying, I hurried over."

Jeff looked around again, feeling cautious.

Mary blinked back the tears that filled her eyes. "I'm a Christian, too."

Mindy looked up in astonishment. Mike stopped what he was doing.

"How do you speak English so well?" Warren asked.

"My father did business in England and Hong Kong when I was a child. He taught our family English."

Jeff noticed the cross hanging from a gold chain around Mary's neck. He couldn't stop looking in her eyes. They were full of life.

"How long have you been a Christian?" Mindy asked.

"Most of my life. My father was very committed. He taught us to pray."

Wonder filled Jeff's heart. "It's incredible how the Lord helped you find us. If we hadn't had that flat tire, we wouldn't have met."

Mary smiled. "It was no accident. God works in all things for good. I pray for China every day of my life. His freedom is coming to my land."

Everyone was sniffling now.

"You must love your father very much," Mindy said. "Is he still alive?"

Mary blinked hard to keep the tears away. "My

father was killed in the Communist Revolution. Chairman Mao's Red Army threw him in prison. They told us it was to re-educate him."

"Why?" Mindy urged.

"He was a Christian land-owner. The government hated landowners and Christians. They took everyone's land away. Mao caused everyone to turn on those who owned anything. Even kids turned on their parents."

Mary paused, gauging how much to tell them.

"My father was tortured in the worst way. When he wouldn't change his mind to renounce God, they shot him. This happened to countless Chinese."

"We're so sorry," Warren said softly.

There wasn't a dry eye in the group. Chen and Jinghau were very quiet. Jeff knew they understood all too well.

He wiped his eyes. "We're here to bring good news to the people of China. We have Bibles."

Mary smiled through her tears. "This is my special day. For months, I've been praying for Bibles. Could you spare some for the people in my village?"

Mike took a deep breath, looking at the others. "We'll give them all to you. It's no accident we're here. You'll know what to do with them. We'll keep the literature for other villages."

Mike explained how they had gotten the Bibles. It was only then that Jeff realized how carefully God had worked to get the Bibles to Mary. He was answering her prayer in an amazing way.

"Can you tell us about the church in China?" Warren asked. "We're very interested."

"Yes," Mary beamed. "Why don't you come to my

home? I'll make you something to drink. We'll just have to be careful not to talk too loud," she cautioned.

Sitting in the tiny one-room house, Jeff couldn't wait to hear the reports. As his eyes scanned Mary's humble dwelling, he got a new grasp on what was important in life.

Tiny chicks, still fuzzy in their infancy, darted across the dirt floor. Hanging from nails driven into the cement walls were framed posters of idealized pagodas, mountain scenes and Chinese opera characters.

Jeff realized this woman didn't value things or wealth, but people. She spent her whole life helping others find the love of God.

Mary gave each of them a cup of tea and a Chinese cookie.

"For hundreds of years," she said, settling right into the discussion, "most Chinese believed in the teachings of Confucius. He was not concerned about life after death, but taught values of goodness related to this life. He believed in the goodness of man and taught a philosophy of great moral truths. You find them in Chinese cookies. In fact, Chinese civilization has survived because of its lofty moral code, even though the code is unaided by divine revelation."

Mindy held up her pencil and writing tablet. "Is it all right if I take notes?"

"Sure," Mary consented. "go ahead.

"For a while," she continued, "some Chinese

strayed into the teachings of Buddhism, with its beliefs of reincarnation and ancestor worship. There was also a strong Christian church. Then came the Communist Revolution."

Everyone leaned forward.

"During the revolution, the Red Guard closed all churches. Whether tiny Gospel halls or large cathedrals, the guard angrily stripped them of every cross. Their hatred for the cross even drove them to chip away all the crosses carved in marble at the entrances of cathedrals."

Jeff sat motionless listening to the shocking history.

Mary spoke powerfully, but without a hateful spirit. "All crosses without exception were destroyed. Under orders from Chairman Mao, the Red Guard even invaded cemeteries throughout China and destroyed gravestones marked by a cross. The cross was the focal point of their hate."

Even as she spoke of such horrible things, Mary smiled. "They could destroy crosses on buildings, but not in hearts. The persecution caused the Chinese Christian church to grow by the millions."

"How could that happen?" Mindy asked.

"When the church buildings were taken away, all missionaries had to leave. It left the church confused. They had to depend on God, and went back to the New Testament model."

"What do you mean?" K.J. asked.

"Small house churches sprang up everywhere, making it hard to stop the sudden growth. Pastors were chosen among the Chinese, and church growth exploded."

"That is so cool," Jeff said. "Maybe the church

will go back to that model in other countries also."

Mary nodded in agreement. "The early church didn't have buildings until three hundred years after it was started. They met in homes."

"Tell us more about the cross," Warren said.

"Now the cross has become the most notable symbol in China," Mary said triumphantly. "In city after city, the crosses on church steeples tower over the fading Red star and any other symbol of a dying Marxist faith. Even Mao's picture, once everywhere, is fast becoming a rarity. Mao's two billion little red books are almost gone, but God's Word is spreading everywhere."

"I'm confused," Mindy said. "If Christianity is growing, why is Communism still in charge, and why are we having so much trouble on this trip? Why did they take away our Bibles?"

Mary smiled. "The leaders of China are very old and confused. They don't know what to do except hold to the old line. Even the peasants and farmers know the Communist experiment was a failure. It's only a matter of time. The cross will completely triumph over everything else."

Jeff's heart was ready to burst. "This country will probably have the largest church in the world. And all this under Communist rule. Do you think this could have happened if China had been a free nation?"

Chen grinned. "It already is the largest church in the world. No one really knows how many Christians there are, but it must be countless millions."

Mary nodded. "Sometimes the church's finest moment is in her darkest hour. I have no doubt

China would have stuck to its old religious ways if there hadn't been persecution."

"Wow," K.J. said.

"What's happening to the strong belief in man's goodness and Confucianism?" Mindy asked.

"The revolution cleaned out a lot of that. Many still hold to those truths, but nothing is spreading as fast as the Gospel. Men of God like Watchman Nee started a new revolution."

Amazed at the stories, the team listened for a while longer to the special way God had worked in the life of this woman and her country. Reluctantly, Jeff looked at his watch. He hated to interrupt, but it was already four o'clock.

"I wonder if Mike got Mindy's tire fixed yet," he said, when there was a break in the conversation. "We need to get to the next village to find a hotel for the night."

"You're welcome to stay here," Mary invited, "but as you can see, I don't have much room."

Jeff was about to respond when Mike walked in. "I think the tire will work now. It's holding air. We need to go to arrive at the hotel by dark."

Mindy took Mary's hands in hers. "I'm so happy for my flat tire—we've been so blessed by the stories. I'll never forget them or you. We'll still be praying for China long after we go home!"

One by one, the rest of the team hugged Mary. Jeff wiped tears from his eyes, knowing he would probably never see her again until heaven. He knew that if they went home now, the whole trip would have been worth it. Mary would place each Bible in the right hands, and the church here would grow.

Mindy walked with Jeff back to the bikes. "I'm really convicted about my attitude before. When I hear stories like that, my problems are so small. Can you imagine? Mary has suffered so much, and she's not even bitter!"

Jeff nodded, grateful for what God had just taught them all.

As they cycled down the highway, Jeff was glad for the cool of the evening. Though the land was still flat in places, the hills were getting harder to climb. Everything was less scenic. The sky was a dull gray like the mountains. The road was paved in some places, but it was mostly covered with gravel and cream-colored dust. Out here, the villages were spread out more. But they were still passing bicycles and tourist buses by the dozen, and the dust was still flying.

"How long will it take to get to the Great Wall tomorrow?" Jeff asked.

"About three hours of riding. It can get a little steep from here on, but the mountain bikes should be great."

K.J. grinned. "I can't wait to get to the Great Wall. I'm going...to get some...incredible footage," he puffed, in between deep breaths.

Jeff smiled, pedaling faster. Looking ahead to the higher mountains, he was overcome with thankfulness. "Thank You, God," he whispered. "Thank You for everything about this day."

Jeff had just turned his attention back to the road

when he heard the hissing sound again. Sure enough, Mindy's patched tire was going flat. He looked over to see her response. She was smiling.

"Hey," she laughed, "I'm not complaining. It's probably another roadside appointment."

Everyone slowed to a stop. Warren got out of the van, while Mike examined the tire. People even came out of their roadside stands to watch.

Mike looked up. "It's leaking again," he said. "And I've already put five patches in that leak."

"It'll be dark soon," Warren reasoned. "The best thing we can do is put the bike in the van and fix it later tonight at the hotel."

"Sounds okay to me," Mindy said. "My leg is starting to cramp up."

Mike nodded. "Even though it's a different size, I might be able to take a tube from the extra bike."

Dawn was breaking as Jeff rolled over in his hotel bed. His mind flashed back to Thursday's events. He couldn't wait to see what would happen today.

After their morning prayer meeting and another breakfast of rice soup, the team prepared to hit the road. Mike and Jeff were just about to head outside when they heard a loud knock on their door. Jeff thought Mindy was playing a game.

"We know it's you, Mindy," Jeff cried. "You can't fool us."

The knock got louder.

Jeff laughed loudly. "Come on, Mindy. It's open."

Jeff's heart skipped a beat. He stared through the open door. It wasn't Mindy.

It was Captain Hu.

Chapter 10

The Great Wall

Jumping to his feet, Jeff felt his body tremble. His mind raced wildly, trying to remember where the literature was. Why hadn't he remembered that Mindy was already back in the room?

Captain Hu pushed the door wide open. "I forbade you to pass out literature," he said loudly. "Yesterday, I received a report from some youth you gave Bibles to."

Jeff didn't know what to say.

Warren walked up. Jeff knew he was restraining himself.

Captain Hu stepped toward him angrily. "I told

you earlier, Mr. Warren. I'm not talking to you. I'm talking to the boy."

Warren was silent, but he didn't step away. Mindy and K.J. crawled further back on the bed they had been sitting on. Chen and Jinghau didn't make a move. Jeff decided to tell the truth.

"We were given some Bibles, sir, and we gave them away."

"I can find out how you got the Bibles, but it really doesn't matter. Didn't I tell you not to give them out?"

Jeff paused, realizing he had made a mistake. Captain Hu just stared at him.

"Sir," Jeff said, breaking the silence, "we believe this is the most important book. People are asking for it."

Captain Hu became angrier. "Who gave you the Bibles?"

Jeff felt sweat building on his brow. "They didn't tell us their names, sir."

"We have ways of finding out," Captain Hu warned.

"You asked me to tell the truth, sir. I'm telling you."

"What did they look like?"

"They were Americans. An older man and a younger man. We saw them for only a few minutes. If I saw them again, maybe I could remember."

Captain Hu put up his hands. "Enough of this. Open your bags. If I find any of your Christian propaganda, you'll suffer severe consequences for breaking the law."

Jeff's heart pounded.

Slowly, the team members emptied their stuff on the bed. Jeff was amazed. Not one piece of literature came out. Everyone had been careful.

Unconvinced, Captain Hu looked at them coldly. "Now, let's have a look in your van. My men will do a search."

Warren handed Captain Hu the keys. Reluctantly, Jeff led Captain Hu to the van.

Mr. Lee was waiting. He searched everything— behind the seats, under the carpet, everywhere. Jeff hoped he wouldn't look in the spare tire panel.

"Where is it?" Captain Hu demanded. "I know it's here."

Jeff prayed for courage. "You've searched the van for yourself. I told you we gave away the Bibles."

Mr. Lee neared the spare tire area.

"Search there," Captain Hu demanded.

Jeff knew they were in trouble now. Mr. Lee pulled out the tire, then the panel. Jeff wanted to close his eyes. Seconds passed like years.

Shaking his head at Captain Hu, Mr. Lee stopped searching. Jeff tried to hide his shock. He wondered if God had blinded their eyes.

Captain Hu looked at him sternly. "I'm going to give you one last warning. If I catch you again, one of my men will guard you for the rest of the trip. Don't forget. I'm watching every move."

Jeff nodded, feeling a great sense of relief. He watched as Captain Hu and Mr. Lee drove off. Then, running as fast as he could, he rejoined the others. He couldn't wait to tell them what had happened.

He burst into the room. "What happened, Warren? Did you hide the stuff?"

Warren grinned. "I'm sorry I didn't tell you. I thought it would be safer that way. Each night, I've been hiding it in a different place."

K.J. shook his head. "This is turning out to be quite a cool story. I can't wait to tell my friends at school."

Everyone laughed.

Jeff gazed at the rugged, dull-gray mountains. As they rode, the villages became more spread out, with farmland stretching between them. The road was steeper now and the air much cooler. Even the Chinese bike riders were riding more slowly, and there were fewer vehicles on the road.

Jeff was glad when Mike motioned for them to stop.

"We're going to shift to a different gear now," Mike directed. "It's going to take some leg power for these last fifteen kilometers."

Mindy took a drink from her water bottle. "You can say that again."

"If anyone gets tired, we can put your bike in the van," Mike reminded them.

Jeff chuckled. "Not me. I've been training for this trip."

Jeff looked ahead, his excitement building. He could already see the Great Wall, one of the greatest construction feats in history. Chen met Jeff's eyes, sharing his excitement even though he had been to the wall many times before.

"How's everybody doing?" Mike asked.

Mindy grimaced. "I'm determined to make it. I'm not a wimp. But it sure is getting cold."

Chen and Jinghau pedaled right along. K.J. and Jeff huffed and puffed.

"I'd like to get some tape of us riding to the Great Wall," K.J. said. "I should probably ride in the van."

"Yeah right, K.J.," Mindy laughed.

Jeff laughed out loud. K.J. stuck out his tongue.

"I think it's a good idea, whether you're tired or not," Jeff said.

Everyone slowed down and let Warren pull up alongside them. K.J. quickly put his bike in the back and grabbed his camcorder.

Then the team continued their slow trek up the hill.

K.J. leaned halfway out the side window to get some good shots.

The team stood at the foot of the mountain where the weathered and gap-toothed wall slithered up. Jeff couldn't believe it. Tourist buses, taxis and bikes filled the busy parking lot. Tourists were everywhere with cameras and camcorders.

Immediately, the team was overwhelmed with Chinese peddlers selling souvenirs and wanting to change money. K.J. loved it and started shooting videotape. It was about two blocks to the base of the Great Wall, and the walk was lined with stalls and shops selling food, drinks and a host of goods.

When the team had chained their bikes to a large post, they headed toward the wall. They tried to remain patient when they were mobbed by more and more peddlers.

"Look at that wall," Jeff exclaimed. "It's incredible. Much more impressive than I thought."

Mindy smiled. "They say it's the only man-made thing visible on the way to the moon."

"Wow," Jeff said.

"Why did they build it?" K.J. asked.

Mindy smiled again. She liked it when the team asked questions. "Nomadic barbarians living to the north were a continual threat. An emperor built it for protection, fearing the Huns of Mongolia."

"How long is it?" K.J. asked.

"You won't believe it—fifteen hundred miles. It's twenty feet tall, with a roadway fifteen feet wide at the top. It's dotted every few hundred yards with a guard tower. At one time, it was manned by a quarter of a million soldiers."

"Boy, Mindy," K.J. said. "How come I don't know this stuff?"

" 'Cause you're the cameraman, and I'm the reporter."

Everyone laughed, especially Jinghau. Jeff could tell she really liked Mindy and the team.

"One more question," K.J. said. "Does anyone know how long it took to build?"

Mindy grinned. "It took over two thousand years to build the major sections of the wall. Then, starting in 221 B.C., over 300,000 men worked for ten years to link it all together."

Jeff jumped in. "I heard it was built wide so five

horses could gallop side by side on the top."

Jinghau nodded. "It was used to convey soldiers, arms and food with amazing speed to various parts of the northern frontier."

K.J. snapped his fingers. "Let's do an interview and get this on tape."

Mike smiled. "That's a good idea. Let's climb up the wall a ways to one of those towers and get some shots from the walkway there. That'll give us a great view of the whole scene."

When they reached a good spot, the team took a few minutes to catch their breath and plan the segment. Doing the shoot was difficult since so many tourists walked along the roadway.

Finally satisfied with the interview, they climbed the steps to the top of the gap-toothed tower to get an even better view. Jeff stood silently for a moment. He could see the wall snaking its way across the tops of the mountains. He closed his eyes. He could almost see in his mind's eye the ancient armies locked in combat, and hear the whistle of arrows and the clang of swords and armor.

Jeff was the last to come down. K.J. was studying the footage in the viewfinder, so Jeff walked along the wall with Warren. After a while, he glanced around to make sure everyone was there. He saw Jinghau, Chen and Mike walking together. But Mindy was nowhere in sight. He rushed over to the others.

"Where's Mindy?"

"We thought she was with you," Mike said.

Jeff whirled around, scanning the crowd. "She's gone."

Chapter 11

Restricted Zone

Jeff was frantic. In a panic, he stared into the sea of faces going by.

"This place is so crowded," he cried. "Maybe she went shopping among all the tourists. You know how she loves shopping."

But no, she wouldn't do that. Jeff ran with Warren along the roadway. He didn't know what to do. His heart thumped thinking that she might have been kidnapped. He tried to fight back the surge of anxiety that threatened to overwhelm him.

"Let's look up there," he said, desperate to start looking. As he and Warren climbed higher up the wall, Jeff prayed.

A half-hour passed. Still no sign.

"What do we do now?" Jeff asked.

Warren responded quickly. "We keep looking. Knowing Mindy, she'll be fine."

It was only two o'clock. Jeff was happy they still had lots of daylight. Craning his neck, he scanned the high towers way up the mountain. An idea hit him. Turning to Warren, he snapped his fingers.

"Mindy is pretty curious. She might have gone up to a higher tower to get a better view."

"That's quite a walk," Warren said.

"You're right," Jeff admitted. "But I'd feel better if we checked."

Warren nodded. He and Jeff ran quickly up the wall to the next tower. Out of breath, they finally arrived. Looking inside, they saw Mindy sitting on a bench with three Chinese girls. She was busy talking about Jesus. Jeff felt angry, but he didn't want to embarrass her. Taking a deep breath, he slowly approached them.

"Jeff," Mindy beamed. "Let me introduce you to my new friends from the university."

Smiling, Jeff hid his frustration. Out of the corner of his eye, he spotted Warren watching. Jeff knew he had to keep his anger under control.

Reaching out his hand, Jeff grinned. "Nice to meet you." Turning to Warren, he unfurled a warm smile. "This is Warren. We've been looking for Mindy. We're glad she's with you."

Mindy hung her head a little. "I'm sorry, Jeff. I had a feeling you might get worried. But when I found out these students speak English, I started telling them about Jesus. They want to know more."

Jeff nodded thoughtfully, feeling bad for interrupting her. "I'll get Jinghau to stay with you for a while. We'll go ahead to find a hotel."

Mindy smiled, grateful her brother and Warren understood.

The youngest student turned to Warren. "My parents manage a very nice hotel a few miles west of here. I'll be glad to call and reserve some rooms for you. We're staying there, too."

Mindy's eyes shone with excitement. Getting a nod from Warren, Jeff realized this was another divine appointment and Mindy was God's tool.

Looking at the Chinese girl, Jeff smiled broadly. "That would be wonderful."

The girl seemed glad. "I'll make the phone call and let them know we'll be there after six."

"Thanks," Jeff said. "We'll go ahead and get the bikes ready. Could you make sure Mindy is at our van in a half-hour?"

"Sure," the girl promised. "We won't be long. We can spend time with her at the hotel."

Jeff realized the impact Mindy had made on the students. A powerful impact for Jesus. Though he would talk to her about it later, he soon forgot that she had broken a club rule and left the group without telling anyone.

Arriving at the old, two-story hotel with a pagoda roof, everyone was amazed as Mindy told about her time with the girls.

"Jiang is the girl whose dad owns the hotel. She wants to hear more about Christianity tonight."

Filled with joy, Jeff and the others carried the luggage to their rooms upstairs.

After dinner, they had a prayer time. Moments after starting, they heard a knock at the door. Everyone looked at each other nervously.

"I'll get it," K.J. offered.

Mindy jumped for joy. It was Jiang. "Come in," she cried. "Please come in."

Jiang walked in shyly. Everyone greeted her as she sat down. She smiled warmly, but her eyes were moist with tears.

"Are you okay?" Mindy asked.

"Yes," she said. "I have been thinking a lot about what you said today. I just wish..."

Suddenly, Jiang burst into uncontrollable sobs.

"What's wrong?" Mindy cried. "Did something happen?"

Jiang wept for a few moments. Everyone sat in stunned silence.

When she was ready, Jiang looked up at everyone. "I'm really sorry. I just wish my older brother could hear about Jesus."

"We'll be glad to tell him, too," Mindy assured her.

Jiang blinked more tears away. "You can't," she said quietly. "He died in the Tiananmen Square massacre in 1989."

Jeff gulped, feeling embarrassed. Yet his heart filled with compassion. "We're very sorry," he stammered.

Mindy and Jinghau each put an arm around Jiang, and the three cried together.

After a while, Jiang wiped her eyes. "My brother's name was Meng. He was one of the strong voices for the students. He wasn't trying to cause trouble, but only wanted some honest talks with the leaders. He believed in democracy and wanted an end to corruption among officials."

She took a deep breath to calm her shaking voice.

"Meng even went on a hunger strike to show his desire for a peaceful solution. After the killing started, he began warning the other students. But late in the night on June 4, he was shot in Tiananmen Square. I stayed with him as he died. My parents don't like to talk about it. But I felt I had to tell you. I'm proud of him. He died for peace."

Tears flowed as Mindy comforted Jiang with an embrace.

When Jiang looked up, her face was a mix of hope and pain. "I wish Meng could have heard about Jesus. He would have been very committed."

Jeff nodded, wiping tears from his own eyes. "Jiang, Jesus died to bring true peace to each of our lives."

She looked at Jeff. "I want to accept Jesus into my heart."

While the group bowed their heads, Mindy led Jiang in the prayer of Salvation. Then Mindy and Jinghau spent the rest of the evening sharing with her and answering her questions before they went to bed. Jeff knew God was at work.

Saturday morning arrived in a hurry. Beams of light streamed across Jeff's room, forcing his weary eyes open. Placing the pillow quickly over his head, he tried to catch a few more winks. But he heard Mike moving about.

"What are you doing so early?" Jeff groaned.

"I need to check the bikes. We're heading back today through Shanxi province, and they need to be in top shape. It'll take me a couple hours."

"I'll come down and help," Jeff volunteered. "But let's get breakfast first."

After eating, Jeff and Mike unchained the bikes. One at a time, Jeff turned them over, watching Mike begin his work like a surgeon.

Mike talked as he worked. "First we'll replace the worn brake pads and tune up the loose gear shifts. After that, we'll take the slack out of the cables and chains."

Jeff watched in wonder. "You know bikes, don't you?"

Mike nodded with confidence. "My love for bikes got me started in this ministry. You wouldn't believe the letters I'm getting from kids asking about these trips."

Jeff grinned. "I hope our video inspires even more kids—that's why I don't mind getting up this early."

Mike laughed. "I know what you mean."

Jeff put grease on the sprockets as Mike directed. Watching Mike work, Jeff knew God had called the right man for the job.

It was ten o'clock when the team prepared to leave. Mindy came outside with Jiang. Both girls beamed with excitement.

"Last night," Mindy said, "Jiang shared with the other girls what happened to her. They're very interested."

"That's wonderful!" Warrren exclaimed.

"I'm going to pray for you every day," Mindy promised Jiang. "And your parents. And your friends. You are the future of China."

Jiang wiped tears from her eyes, hugging Mindy and the rest of the team good-bye.

Pedaling down the dusty road, Jeff was lost in his own thoughts. He was thinking about how exciting it was to see God at work firsthand, when he spotted a village to the left. He noticed how different it looked from the scores of villages they had seen. Huge factory buildings with smoke stacks shot into the sky. Everything was dirty and crammed close together.

"Mike," Jeff called out, "maybe we should stop here."

"Sure. But let's set a time limit. We still have to go another twenty kilometers today." Mike slowed a little, glancing at his watch. "Let's stay until lunchtime. The ride will be easier—even downhill some of the way."

Jeff and the others nodded with excitement.

Pulling off the main highway, they pedaled down a dirt road leading to the village. Close up, Jeff saw how drab and dull everything looked. Scanning the landscape, he prayed for God to open doors.

After stopping, the team divided into two

groups. Jeff's group shared with several older Chinese people sitting on benches along the road. Bikers passed by, as well as some trucks. The sounds of bells and honking horns seemed to never end.

All too quickly, their time was up and everyone headed back to the van. After they shared for a few minutes, Mike gave instructions for the afternoon ride. Jeff was glad they would ride only an hour before lunch.

As they prepared to leave, two red landrovers appeared out of nowhere. They raced toward the team. Jeff looked closer, his heart pounding.

It was the police—again!

Chapter 12

The New Rider

Jeff was sure it was Captain Hu. But scanning the landrovers, he saw that the captain wasn't with them.

The vehicles skidded to a halt. Rushing out of the jeeps, six angry men stood guard around the team. Jeff realized the men probably didn't speak English.

Stunned and confused, Jeff turned to Warren. "This must be some kind of misunderstanding. We haven't done anything wrong."

The man in charge talked with Chen and Jinghau in Mandarin. After a few minutes, Chen turned to the team.

"They're saying we're in a restricted area.

They're probably right. This village is off limits to visitors. I'm sorry. I should have known this."

Jeff frowned. "Tell them we're sorry and that we'll leave right away."

Chen translated what Jeff said into Mandarin. Everyone waited while Chen and Jinghau talked with the leader. Finally, the brother and sister gave up.

"They're not letting us go," Jinghau reported. "They're holding us until Captain Hu gives further orders."

Mindy groaned. "I knew I'd end up in a Chinese prison."

"Remember, Mindy," K.J. grinned, "God may want to use you there."

In that moment, Mindy made a decision. "Well, if that's what He wants, I'm willing."

"I'm just kidding, Mindy," K.J. said. "It was just a joke."

Hearing Mindy's words, Jeff was proud. He had never heard her speak with such commitment. He knew she meant business for God.

Everyone sat on the grass nearby, waiting. K.J. was really quiet.

"What do you think they'll do with us?" Jeff asked.

"If Captain Hu comes, this trip is over," Jinghau said simply.

"That's for sure," Jeff said. "That's for sure."

An hour passed. At one o'clock, Jeff saw another

red landrover driving toward them. From a distance, Jeff saw two passengers.

Straining his eyes, he looked closer. "We're in trouble now," he cried. "It's Captain Hu."

"And Mr. Lee," K.J. moaned.

The jeep jerked to a halt. The men were clearly angry. They purposefully stepped down from the jeep.

Captain Hu looked furiously at the team. "You have given me no choice but to take serious action."

"We didn't know this was a restricted zone," Jeff protested.

Captain Hu laughed coldly. "You should have known." He looked sternly at Warren, then addressed his question to Jeff. "What do you think I should do with you, young man?"

Jeff hung his head. "I don't know, sir. We're all sorry."

"I'm tired of you being sorry. I have more reason than I need to arrest you or throw you out of the country."

The team waited quietly while Captain Hu dismissed everyone except Mr. Lee. After the men drove away, Captain Hu walked slowly around the bikes.

"These are nice. Where did you get them?"

"My friends rented them in Beijing," Jeff said, feeling that something was weird about Captain Hu's behavior.

"Enough of this," Captain Hu said abruptly. "I've decided what I'm going to do. I'm going to put you under arrest."

Jeff felt sick. "What do you mean, sir?"

"You will finish your trip under arrest. Mr. Lee is a good rider. He will travel with you at all times. I will be in radio communication with him. You must do what he says."

The team members almost smiled. This wasn't good news, but it was better than prison.

The captain glared. "Don't try anything foolish. This is your last chance. Next time I'll confiscate your bikes and put you in jail. Is that understood?"

Everyone nodded.

Captain Hu barely waited for Mr. Lee to lift a shiny mountain bike out of the jeep before driving off.

Jeff stared at Mr. Lee. He gave Jeff a disgusted look back. "One wrong move, and you'll be in serious trouble."

"Yes, sir," Jeff said.

"What are your travel plans?" Mr. Lee demanded.

"If you don't mind," Jeff said, "we're going to bike for an hour and then get some lunch."

"Fine," Mr. Lee said. "But stay in my sight. Ask permission wherever you go."

Jeff nodded slowly. This was going to be a tense ride.

Climbing onto their bike seats, the team headed out. Soon, they crossed into the province of Shanxi. Though mountainous, the ride was not as difficult as the journey to the Great Wall had been. Most of the time they traveled downhill.

Everyone stayed close together. Mr. Lee rode in front with Jeff and Mike. Jeff felt frustrated, knowing they couldn't pass out literature or witness. Though grateful for the divine appointments along the way, he hoped God had more. But they were being watched now. Perhaps they could get through to Mr. Lee.

Sitting in a small restaurant much like the one they went to the first day of the ride, Jeff and the others ate their lunch of noodles and rice. Mr. Lee sat at another table, hardly looking their way.

Determined to make an effort, Jeff walked over to him. "Are you sure you wouldn't like to join us?"

Mr. Lee shook his head with a flare of anger.

Reluctantly, Jeff sat back down at his own table. Suddenly, he snapped his fingers and whispered.

"I've got an idea."

Chapter 13

A Secret Plan

Everyone stared at Jeff in anticipation.

"What's your idea?" Mindy teased. "Are you going to make Mr. Lee disappear?"

"This I have to see," K.J. added.

Jeff ran his fingers through his dusty blond hair. "You're not too far off, Mindy."

"Don't be funny, Jeff," Mindy laughed. "I believe in prayer, but making a man vanish in thin air?"

K.J.'s eyes grew big.

"Listen, you guys," Jeff said seriously. "We still have some literature, and one piece could change a whole village. Here's my idea. Mike and I will ride real fast in front. Chen and Jinghau will ride in the middle. K.J. and Mindy will start complaining about tiredness and drop back a ways into the other bikers. In the confusion, we'll get far enough apart so you can give some literature out as we go through villages."

K.J. laughed. "Making him vanish will be easier. He'll catch on."

"No," Mike said. "Jeff's right. Another team did the same thing. If Mr. Lee figures it out, then we'll change our plan."

"I'd like to talk to him about the Lord," Mindy said. "I don't want to make him mad at us."

Mike nodded thoughtfully. "That's a good point, Mindy. But I think we need to go ahead and test the plan today. We'll give out literature tomorrow if it works."

After lunch, Jeff and Mike followed the plan. Since Mr. Lee was a good rider, he had no problem keeping up with the speeding pair. At first, everyone kept up with them.

Finally, Mindy called out. "My leg's sore, Jeff. Slow it down."

K.J. jumped in. "Yeah. Cool it, you guys."

Jeff yelled back. "We need to keep moving. Try to keep pace. You can catch up if you get behind."

Jeff looked at Mr. Lee, who just kept pedaling. Slowly the gap grew as Mindy and K.J. started dragging behind. Warren passed them in the van to give them cover. Jeff and Mike sped up even faster.

Quickly, Mr. Lee pedaled faster, not wanting to show any weakness in riding.

"You like riding, don't you, Mr. Lee?" Jeff asked.

"It's okay," he responded.

Jeff kept talking. At first, Mr. Lee hardly said a word. But soon, he started answering Jeff's questions more completely. As time passed, Jeff learned all about Mr. Lee, and the policeman started warming up. Jeff was amazed.

In the meantime, K.J. and Mindy lagged further and further behind.

Mr. Lee turned around to check their progress. "We better stop for a few minutes. The others need a rest."

Jeff realized the plan had worked. It just needed more time. They would try again later and put it into full action on Sunday.

That evening, Mr. Lee joined them for dinner at the hotel. After ordering the food, the tired team sat quietly. Jeff knew God loved Mr. Lee, and he didn't want to miss an opportunity. As he opened his mouth to share, Mindy beat him to it.

"What do you think of us, Mr. Lee?" she asked.

Mr. Lee frowned. "It is not my job to give my opinion. My job is to keep an eye on you."

Mindy smiled anyway, her braces gleaming from the ceiling light. "Mr. Lee," she said, "we love China. We're sorry we've been such a problem for Captain Hu."

Mr. Lee looked skeptical. "Lots of groups like

yours come to China. They all want to save our country."

"Is that bad?" Mindy asked.

Mr. Lee shrugged. The food arrived, and everyone started eating.

After a quick bite, Mindy looked at Mr. Lee. "Do you believe in God?"

Jeff almost gulped.

Mr. Lee stared at her coldly. "Don't try to convert me," he said sternly. "I don't need your God."

Mindy's face turned red. But she looked him right in the eye. "I'm sorry, Mr. Lee. But I love God so much I want to tell others about Him."

"How do you know there is a God?" Mr. Lee hissed.

Jeff almost cheered. If this wasn't an open door, there would never be one. He looked down at his plate, lifting the noodles to his mouth and praying.

Mindy knew Mr. Lee had asked a key question, even if he had asked it angrily. She put down her fork. "I know there is a God because He changed my life."

Mr. Lee tried to ignore her. But Mindy went on to tell him how she met Jesus, and how God sent His Son. And why.

Jeff looked at Mr. Lee in amazement. He was starting to listen. K.J. was praying between every bite of Chinese food. Chen and Jinghau and Mike and Warren were busy eating, too. But Jeff knew they were all praying that Mindy would get through.

Mindy tried to answer Mr. Lee's hard questions. After a while, Mr. Lee became uncomfortable. He stood up abruptly, making a show of looking at his watch.

"I'm sorry," he said gruffly. "I'm going to have to ask you to return to your rooms now. Please don't leave unless you call. I'll be in the room next door."

Warren smiled. He knew it would be a great time to have a prayer meeting.

As soon as Mr. Lee went into his room, the team gathered for prayer.

"God has really given me lots of love for this man," Mindy said. "I believe we're sowing seeds of truth into his life that he'll never forget."

Warren smiled. "You're right, Mindy. After experiencing nothing but the coldness of Communism in his life, he sees something real in us. Let's pray that he sees the reality he's been looking for."

Jeff looked troubled. "Should we still go ahead with our plan tomorrow?"

"Good question," Mindy said. "What if he catches on? He won't think much of us then."

Warren looked at Mike, leaving the decision to him.

"We'll try it tomorrow at the beginning," Mike decided. "Then we'll have the rest of the trip to talk with him. The key thing is prayer. Let's pray for him."

The team gathered in a circle. After joining hands, Jeff looked up. With Chen on one side of him and Jinghau on the other, his heart suddenly filled with love for the Chinese people. Tears flooded his eyes as he saw a picture in his mind.

He spoke softly. "I just saw the most beautiful picture of what heaven will be like. Heaven won't be just Americans or Westerners. It'll be people from every tribe, nation and tongue. Perhaps the greatest number of people will be Chinese."

Several of the group wiped tears from their eyes. Jeff went on.

"Jesus died for all mankind. He has the power to break Communism and darkness in this huge nation of over one billion people."

"Let's pray," Warren said. "God wants to touch Mr. Lee."

Everyone bowed their heads. Jeff felt love so real and powerful. He was glad he was part of a team of real kids.

"Lord," Jeff cried, "I'm so full of your love right now. If I feel it this strongly, I can't imagine how much you love the Chinese people. Please release power across this land. Let their sufferings turn to salvation."

"And, Lord," Mindy prayed, "I know You love Mr. Wan Lee. Please let him see Your love in our hearts."

Everyone said amen.

Golden rays of sunshine poured into the rooms, announcing Sunday morning. Since Jeff's window faced east, the sun hit him with full strength. Opening his eyes, he looked around. The others were sound asleep. Quietly, he dressed, deciding to go for a prayer walk. Slipping outside, he walked around the hotel, looking out at the nearby village. He knew he had to stay near the hotel. But he prayed and rejoiced, walking the land he now loved.

After breakfast, the team gathered together at the van. Though Mr. Lee watched them closely, Jeff noticed a different look on his face. Mindy and Jeff went to greet him.

"Good morning, Mr. Lee," Mindy said, brightly. "How are you doing today?"

Mr. Lee hesitated to answer.

"Are you okay?" Mindy asked gently.

Finally, Mr. Lee looked up. "Well...I never thought I would say this...and I risk a lot by talking about it, but you've got me thinking."

Chapter 14

The Attack

Mr. Lee cleared his throat, wanting to talk, but clearly nervous.

"My greatest hero was Chairman Mao," he said at last. "As a very young man, I gave everything to follow him. But his dream for China was never realized. Since then, I've been loyal to the party but have had lots of questions. So many people were hurt or killed, and our nation isn't any better."

A haunted look crossed his face.

"I was part of the army that crushed the university students' demonstration at Tiananmen Square. I've felt guilty about the killing of so many in cold blood. Maybe the students were right."

Jeff was in a state of shock. He and Mindy were listening to the confession of a radical Communist.

Mr. Lee looked at them searchingly. "If anybody finds out I said this, I'll be put in prison. But, I've watched all of you. And especially you, Mindy. I know you believe in something real. I can see it in your eyes. And you have so much joy. I never knew that kind of joy when I was your age. It has to be real. And I've been watching your video. What you said last night kept me awake. Can you give me anything to read that will help me?"

With a sinking feeling, Jeff realized it was a trap. Captain Hu must have told Mr. Lee to trick them. Was this his final scheme to nail them?

Looking at the others, Jeff wondered what to do. Suddenly, he had an idea. Reaching inside the van, he pulled out his personal Bible, which was legal to have. "I want to give you a special gift. It's my personal Bible. As you read it, it will answer all your questions about life."

Mr. Lee took it, thumbing slowly through the pages. Everyone waited hopefully.

At last, Mr. Lee looked up with a grateful smile. "Thank you very much, Jeff. I don't know if I can take this." He started to hand the Bible back.

Jeff put his hands up. "Please. I want to give it to you. I just hope it doesn't get you in trouble."

"If Captain Hu heard me now, I'd be in real trouble."

"We won't say a word," Mindy assured him.

Mr. Lee looked at the team with a trace of amusement. "By the way, your tricky plan to pass out literature hasn't fooled me. I knew what you were doing and was about to call Captain Hu. Now I don't know what to do."

Jeff blushed. "We're sorry about that. Let me be totally honest with you. We have a few pieces of literature left. If you want them, we'll give them to you."

Mr. Lee was making a difficult decision. "Look, I could be severely punished for this. But if you want to try your secret plan today, then fine. Just don't get me in trouble. My life is on the line."

Everyone nodded soberly. Jeff wanted to pray with him, but felt he should wait. He wanted to make sure Mr. Lee completely understood the Gospel.

The team had been biking for two hours when Jeff realized he hadn't noticed any of the scenery around him. All morning, he and Mike had ridden in front with Mr. Lee. Jeff spent a lot of time with him, trying to answer his questions. He couldn't believe how God had prepared Mr. Lee's heart. It was like a story from the Book of Acts.

Mindy had really wanted to ride up front so she could share, but everybody felt it best that she and K.J. fall back. Even now, Mindy and K.J. were way behind the team. Spotting a group of people in front of a village that bordered the road, Mindy carefully pulled out a handful of literature. Looking around, she handed some to a young couple, then some to an old man. They stayed as long as they dared, then raced to pass Warren in the van and take their place behind Chen and Jinghau.

"K.J.," Mindy urged when they had been riding with the team for a while. "Let's do it again. I have five pieces of literature left."

"Sounds good to me," he agreed.

Slowly, they trailed behind. This time they were passing through a village crowded with factory buildings and bustling with people. Gradually, they fell way behind.

"Look," K.J. said, pointing. "There's a smaller group of people alongside the road. Let's give them some."

After uttering a quick prayer, they handed out the literature. Suddenly, Mindy gasped, looking to her right side.

"Look!" she cried. "It's Captain Hu."

Hidden behind a factory building was a red landrover. Captain Hu just sat there, staring at them.

"What do we do now?" K.J. wailed.

"Let's just ride past him like nothing is wrong and get back to the others quickly."

Racing as fast as their legs could pedal, they finally caught up.

"I don't want to tell the others," Mindy worried. "It will freak everybody out."

"We have to tell them," K.J. said. "It'll mean curtains for Mr. Lee if we don't."

Just as they were going to reveal what they had seen, Captain Hu sped by wildly, almost hitting them.

Jeff looked back, shaken and stunned. "That guy almost ran us over. It looks like a landrover used by Captain Hu's men."

"Jeff," Mindy cried, pedaling closer. "That was Captain Hu himself. I hate to tell you, but he saw us passing out literature back there. He was hiding."

"Oh no," Jeff moaned. "I'm sure he's on his way to get a big police wagon to arrest us all."

Mr. Lee looked troubled. "It will probably be for me, too."

Everyone rode quietly through the village for the next few minutes, not knowing what to do. Jeff felt helpless, like someone had hit him with a giant board, like they were riding into a giant trap. Anytime, they would find out their fate.

Jeff spotted the red landrover first. It was heading right at them. He could see Captain Hu driving.

"What shall we do?" Mindy pleaded.

"Keep riding," Jeff directed. "Act like nothing is wrong."

"And stay together," Mike added.

Captain Hu sped crazily toward them, moving to the side of the road where they were riding. Horns blared. Villagers stared in disbelief.

"Look out!" Mike cried. "He's trying to hit us."

The team rode as close to the edge of the road as they could, forming a single file row. They braced for the worst, forcing themselves to keep their eyes open.

Jeff screamed as a strong, terrifying gust from the passing landrover almost blew him off the road.

"That was close," Chen cried. "I hope he doesn't hit Warren."

Jeff looked back, seeing Captain Hu just miss the van.

"He's trying to kill us," Mindy sobbed.

Before they could act, they heard the roar of an approaching engine. This time, the landrover was lined up right behind them.

"He's crazy," Mike said, completely baffled.

Jeff looked straight ahead. The roaring sound was almost upon them. He knew they had to make a choice. Either pull off to the side of the road and crash into the potholes and buildings, or stay on the road. He couldn't believe Captain Hu would really run them down.

Jeff kept waiting for the captain to slam on the brakes. Looking out of the corner of his eye, he saw Mindy riding dangerously close to the edge of the road. The landrover was on her tail, and she was losing control.

"Jeff," she screamed, "I'm gonna..."

Jeff saw Mindy hit a pothole and career out of control toward a roadside building.

K.J.'s eyes were wild with fear. Captain Hu kept coming. Straight at them. Jeff knew that at any second the landrover would smash into them.

Jeff shuddered. Would this be how they would die?

Chapter 15

Detained

Jeff heard the sound of screaming, screeching tires. He opened his eyes just in time to see Captain Hu swerve around the team. Scarcely believing they were all still alive, everyone pulled on their brakes. Mindy lay sprawled alongside the road. Villagers came running to see what had happened.

Captain Hu got out of his jeep, laughing at their fear. But only for a moment. Then he began yelling. "I gave you orders not to pass out literature. Do you not understand the word *forbidden?*"

Everyone except K.J. sat frozen on their bike saddles. He had already jumped off to help Mindy. By now, Warren had pulled up and was running to Mindy's side, too.

"Leave her alone," Captain Hu demanded.

"She's hurt," Warren protested.

Captain Hu's eyes darkened with rage. "I said leave her alone."

Warren and K.J. backed off. Slowly, Mindy got up, hobbling toward the others. Jeff winced when he saw her scraped arms and legs. He wanted to help her, but he didn't dare make a move.

Captain Hu looked angrily at Mr. Lee. "I'm surprised you weren't aware of their little tricks. They fooled you all morning, and I saw it all. I should have put somebody more competent out here. We don't train our people like we used to."

Mr. Lee took a step back. "I'm sorry, sir. I guess they outsmarted me."

Moments passed like years. Jeff and the others pulled their bikes off to the side of the road while Captain Hu went back to his landrover radio to make a call. Jeff knew he wouldn't let them go this time.

Jeff wondered if they had pushed the rules too far. He also wondered why Captain Hu had such a strong dislike for them.

The team sat on the roadside for at least fifteen minutes. The bike tour had come to an abrupt end. Jeff was happy that much of the video had been shot. He hoped Captain Hu wouldn't take their equipment.

He looked at the frightened team. By now, Warren had slipped the first aid kit to Mindy. She was bandaging her arms and legs.

They all saw it at the same time. A dump truck

was coming down the road, escorted by another police landrover.

"Uh oh," Chen said. "I think that's for us."

Captain Hu strode toward them, motioning them to their feet. "This time," he announced, "I'm putting you under real arrest."

Jeff didn't want to hear those words. But he knew they had been caught red-handed passing out literature. Their fate would be in God's hands.

He watched the dump truck pull to the side of the road. The driver noisily opened the back gate.

"Put your bikes inside," Captain Hu commanded.

Warren nodded for them to obey. One by one the mountain bikes were lifted up and pushed to the front of the dump truck.

Captain Hu scowled at Warren. Jeff knew he didn't like him. "You first," he ordered. "Get in."

Jeff had to say something. "What about the van? We can't leave it here."

"You will leave it here," Captain Hu yelled. "Don't tell me what you can't do."

Jeff took a step back, knowing to be quiet. He imagined what it must have been like to be arrested during the Communist Revolution. It would have been a lot worse than a dump truck. It would have meant torture or even death.

Surely that wouldn't happen now!

"The rest of you get in," Captain Hu ordered. "You have a long ride to the Beijing jail. Mr. Lee will personally guard you in the back."

Nobody could see anything as they bounced along in the back of the truck. The rough ride was not what their sore muscles needed.

"I hope you won't get in trouble," Jeff shouted above the noise.

"So do I," Mr. Lee said. "He seems to believe you guys were tricking me. If that's true, I'll get a strong warning and reprimand. But if I do get in trouble, then that's the way it goes. Something's happening in my heart. I see things clearer now."

Jeff looked over at Mike and Warren. They both nodded to "go for it." Jeff knew what to do next.

"Do you mind if we pray with you?" he asked. "We may never see you again once we get to Beijing. I know it seems fast, but would you consider asking Jesus into your heart? He's the true Chairman of our lives."

Mr. Lee paused, then nodded yes. "I don't really have anything to lose, do I?"

Everyone beamed with excitement.

"This is worth the whole trip," Mindy said, suddenly feeling the pain of her cuts. "Even my fall from the bike is worth this."

"I can't believe Captain Hu put you back here," K.J. said. "It seems so stupid."

"He's angry with me. I failed in my job. This is his way of punishing me. But I don't really trust him. Something is wrong with that man, and I'm not the only one who's concerned."

Jeff wanted to ask what he meant, but he knew it was time to pray. He put his hand on Mr. Lee's shoulder. "Please pray after me."

"Lord Jesus, I realize You are the only Savior and the ruler of the universe."

Mr. Lee repeated the words.

"I'm sorry for all my sins. I'm especially sorry for killing innocent people in Tiananmen Square."

Mr. Lee repeated after Jeff, beginning to weep as he prayed.

"Please forgive me and cleanse me from all my wrongdoing. Come into my heart. I want you to be the new Chairman of my life."

Jeff waited for him to finish. Afterward, everyone rejoiced at how God had revealed Himself to Mr. Lee.

Jeff hugged Mr. Lee, laughing through his tears. "Boy, if Captain Hu could see us now."

Mr. Lee smiled at the love they showed him. But something troubled him. "What will I do when you're gone?"

Jeff looked him in the eye. "We may never see you again, but God will never leave you. Read the Bible I gave you. Find some believers to fellowship with. This decision is going to cost you, but the Truth of God now lives in your heart."

Everyone rejoiced. Even on the way to jail.

As they bounced along the busy, noisy streets of Beijing, Jeff wondered how they were going to get out of this jam. He had seen God come through so many times before. Jeff had slain his bears and his lions. He had seen some giants fall too.

They all took a deep breath as the dump truck pulled into the large police headquarters and jerked to a full stop. A policeman opened the back gate. Jeff was surprised to see the van pull in behind them, driven by one of Captain Hu's men.

Captain Hu stepped into sight. "Get out," he demanded. "Get out now."

Everyone slowly moved to the gate, jumping two by two to the ground.

"Now follow me," he ordered.

Jeff and the others obeyed. The whole time they walked, Captain Hu reprimanded Mr. Lee. As they entered the headquarters, Jeff found himself praying again and again that God would protect his new brother in the Lord.

Captain Hu took them to a questioning room, then left like a parent leaving his children to think about what they'd done wrong. Finally he returned.

"What do you think of your club now?" he asked, falling into his old pattern of addressing Jeff. He seemed to enjoy picking on him.

"We're sorry we've been such a big problem," Jeff said.

"*Sorry*. You should have been sorry the first time I saw you. Now you'll be spending time in our lovely prison."

Jeff felt the words cut like a knife to his spirit.

Captain Hu went on. "Not only that, but you've really messed it up for Chen and Jinghau. Their university days are over, and they could be in jail for years for treason against our country."

Chen and Jinghau didn't move a face muscle. Jeff knew the peace of God was on them.

"We're scheduled to catch a plane tomorrow," Jeff said.

Captain Hu thought this was funny. "Right," he

laughed. "You're going to start your prison stay tonight."

Mindy shivered even though it was hot in the room.

Captain Hu nodded at Chen and Jinghau with a look of disdain. "We finished off kids like you in 1989. You're deceived. You think you have answers for the future. You're wrong. You'll have to be re-educated."

Jeff didn't like those words. "We demand to see a representative from the American embassy."

Captain Hu was immovable. "The only thing you'll see is the bars of our jail."

"What charges are you bringing against us?" Jeff demanded.

Captain Hu looked at his men and snickered. Mr. Lee sat still and didn't say a word.

"I'm charging you with speaking against the government and passing out anti-government propaganda."

"And what about Chen and Jinghau? They haven't done anything wrong. They were translators. They didn't pass out any literature."

Captain Hu walked up to Chen and pushed him against the wall. "To start with, they're charged with stealing bikes."

"They didn't steal any bikes," Jeff cried, "and you know it."

Captain Hu laughed. "We have ways of sending people to prison for a long time."

Chapter 16

Wheels of Fortune

Jeff's heart sank as Captain Hu left the room. The last thing he wanted was to be responsible for sending Chinese Christians to prison. But what could he do now?

Chen and Jinghau couldn't hide their discouragement any longer. They knew Captain Hu had the power to put them away.

"We're sorry," Mindy said with tears rolling down her face. "If we would have known this would happen, we would have never asked you to help."

Jinghau wept. But when she looked up, peace shined through her tears. "Please don't feel sad. This has been the most wonderful trip of my life. If we go to jail for our faith or lose our rights to go to university, then we'll rejoice with God's grace."

K.J. became angry. "How can he make up a story like that? He knows you didn't steal any bikes."

Chen sighed. "You can't imagine what has happened in the past to people who think differently than the government. Many are still being persecuted. Many still sit in prison. Some have even died."

Jeff wanted to say something encouraging, but before he thought of anything, a group of policemen rushed in. One by one, the team members were escorted to the old prison.

Jeff was the last to go. When he got there, he looked around, preparing for a long night. The first thing he noticed was that Chen and Jinghau had been separated from the club. The second thing he noticed were the bars—rusty and cold-looking. The cell was pretty large, big enough for the five Americans to spend an uncomfortable night. He was thankful that he wouldn't have to spend the night alone. But it worried him that Chen and Jinghau had been taken to another part of the prison.

Jeff awoke on his cot, missing the flood of sunshine that had greeted him every other morning of the trip. He had hoped to wake up and find that Sunday had all been a dream. But it was not a dream. And it was not what he had planned.

The others were already awake. Jeff was surprised that any of them had slept at all.

Mindy sat on her cot, her chin in her hands. "We're supposed to fly out tonight. I guess that won't be happening."

"I'm not so concerned about us," Mike said. "I can't get Jinghau and Chen off my mind. I would do anything to get them out of this mess."

"Me, too," K.J. sighed.

"God is bigger than Captain Hu," Warren offered.

For the next few minutes, the team prayed together. Trying to stir his faith, Jeff joined them. Finally, everyone sat in silence.

Hours later, Jeff stared at the floor, still sitting on his cot. Suddenly, the cell door swung open. It was Mr. Lee.

"Are they putting you in here, too?" Jeff asked in dismay.

Mr. Lee shook his head.

"Why are you here then?"

"We need you to answer some questions."

Jeff looked confused. "We have nothing to add to what you already know."

Mr. Lee allowed himself to smile. He had very good news for his friends, even if it was bad news for the police. "Captain Hu has gotten himself into some serious trouble. It seems he's not the committed Communist we all thought he was. We just found out that he's been stealing bikes and other things from visitors like you. A number of our men have been questioned, and the pieces are fitting together."

Jeff was shocked. "You mean he was selfish and greedy like the rest of the world."

"That's right," Mr. Lee said. "I can see now why a government change won't do it for a nation. Change must come from the heart."

"But what about us?" Mindy asked. "We broke the law. Aren't they going to punish us?"

"I've talked with my leaders. Legally, they could make you serve a short prison term for breaking our laws. But they're more embarrassed about the way Captain Hu treated you. I think he was at the breaking point."

Jeff took a deep breath. "Why do they want to question us?"

"They want you to share how Captain Hu tried to run you down. That is not the way we treat our guests, no matter what they've done."

Joy shone in Mr. Lee's eyes, even as he tried to maintain his professionalism for anyone who might be watching. "Captain Hu's boss sends his personal apology. After questioning, you will be free to go. Captain Hu is the one who may be going to prison."

K.J. had to restrain himself to keep from shouting. Jeff and Mindy hugged. Then Mindy looked up at Mr. Lee.

"What about Chen and Jinghau?"

"They will be released to go back to university. They'll be watched very closely in the next few months, but nothing should happen to them. You can see them in a few minutes."

Jeff smiled, remembering how attached he had become to them. They had become much more than translators.

"What about you, Mr. Lee?" K.J. asked.

"I'll be okay," he said. Then he paused. "Thanks to you, I have the Truth I've searched for all my life."

Jeff thought of Jiang and the other university girls. He knew they would sow seeds of light and truth. He thought of all the others they had met along the way. Of Mary, and how she loved the precious Word. Then he looked up at Mr. Lee.

Mr. Lee's eyes sparkled. Jeff saw something in those eyes he would never forget.

His eyes spoke of the future. A bright future. They revealed a future mystery, that someday soon Communism, not Christianity, would be the closed road. The forbidden road.